BECOMING ADULT,
BECOMING CHRISTIAN

Becoming Adult, Becoming Christian

Adult Development and Christian Faith

JAMES W. FOWLER

Harper & Row, Publishers, San Francisco

Cambridge, Hagerstown, New York, Philadelphia
London, Mexico City, São Paulo, Singapore, Sydney

FIRST EDITION

Library of Congress Cataloging in Publication Data

Fowler, James W., 1940-
    BECOMING ADULT, BECOMING CHRISTIAN.

    Includes index.
    1. Faith—Psychology. 2. Adulthood—Psychological aspects. 3. Developmental psychology. 4. Christian life—1960-   . I. Title.
BT771.2.F65 1984   248.8′4   83-48987
ISBN 0-06-062841-3

84 85 86 87 88   10 9 8 7 6 5 4 3 2 1

TO

JAMES LUTHER ADAMS
and
CARLYLE MARNEY

Mentors and Exemplars in Vocation

Contents

Introduction

A man gazed out the window of his study. The flashing red of two cardinals played against green holly branches sagging under the wet February snow. Memories of those whose lives had touched his and made a difference brought tears to his eyes. He was in anguish; he prayed for help. Two paths lay open before him. He was standing on the edge of middle age: the choice seemed a big one. One path led to institutional leadership and administrative challenge. It also promised to fulfill the boyhood dream his parents had implanted. The other involved finishing a half-written book and continuing the rigors of research, teaching, and writing—confirming the tasks and channels of influence that had emerged, unbidden, in his thirties. He could not take both paths. One had to be chosen, the other rejected, a dream denied.

What *should* he do? What did *he* what? What did *God* want? Who or what cause was he willing to disappoint? Motives of destiny and calling twined together in his mind and heart in a perplexing mix.

For this man, as for each of us, questions of destiny and calling lay at the heart of his unfolding story as an adult. He wanted to be a Christian; he wanted to align his life with the will of God. At the same time he was a man of his era, filled with amibition and hope, charged with the drive to self-actualization and to the fulfillment of his destiny.

In the course of a few days he made his choice. He opted for continuity. He affirmed the emergent directions of his thirties and recommitted himself to writing, research, and teaching. He made a phone call that amputated the other future.

Peace did not come immediately. In succeeding months, periods of struggle, pain, and doubt disturbed him. Destiny and vocation, he discovered, run deep into our psyches and our faith. They connect our images of ourselves and of God. They also profoundly affect our relations with those who are nearest and dearest to us.

When he had completed his book, he turned to a new agenda. From his reflections and learnings through his mid-life wrestle with vocation, he sensed that our society and our churches are poorly equipped to help people deal with adult development and destiny, with vocation and faith. Without being autobiographical, he began to write a personal book. Without directly telling his own story, he found himself writing about the crisis of vocational ideals in our society. Without making it a confessional, he found himself mining the richness of biblical faith for images and orientation characterizing partnership with God.

When the book was finished, he called it *Becoming Adult, Becoming Christian*.

I. Adult Development Theories and the Crisis of Vocation

1. THE CRISIS IN VOCATIONAL IDEALS

The Shorter Westminster Catechism begins with this question: "What is the chief end of man?" Its answer, learned by twenty generations of the theological heirs of John Calvin, states, "The chief end of man is to glorify God and to enjoy Him forever."[1] This is a *vocational* question. It asks, What are human beings here for? In what consists the virtue or the excellence of human beings? In what pursuits, attainments, or investments will human beings find deepest fulfillment? In what modes of living, of spending, and being spent will humans realize their full potential and contributions?

A vital key to understanding any society consists in examining the range of vocational ideals that it recognizes and to which it nurtures its members. For tight-knit societies like Calvin's Geneva (or the Scottish villages where the Westminster Catechism has been taught for hundreds of years), one central vocational ideal may have been enough. This would be true particularly for those who, like Calvin, partook deeply in the belief in a sovereign, yet merciful God. But consider some other cultural vocational ideals. In Aristotle's *Nichomachean Ethics* we encounter the image of the *Megalopsychos,* the "high-minded man," whose virtues, habits of taste, and artistry in friendship and public life made him truly worthy of respect and emulation. The Stoics offered the image of the rational man, who avoids excesses of passion through the alignment of his reason with the rational structures of the universe. Early Christianity offered vocational models of the disciple and the martyr, not to mention the life centered in the love of God and neighbor exemplified by the Christ. Later Christianity generated a variety of vocational ideals from the eremitic monastics to laypeople devoted, even in marriage, to celibacy and chastity. When the divine right of kings found new forms in Europe as a rationale for royal authority, there emerged with it vocational ideals of the Christian prince. In the eleventh century, with the shaping of a language and the ideals of courtly, romantic love, the vocational ideal of the courtier began to take form. Among the knights-templar of the Crusades, a vocational ideal of the "soldier-saint became vital, and in many guises it has reappeared regularly in Western nations. In Eastern societies we see, in many forms, the vocational ideals of the sage, the monastic, the bureaucratic statesman; in Japan we see an Eastern version of the ideal of the soldier-saint, the Samurai.

As this brief listing of examples suggests, a society's values, its narrative structures of meaning, and its range of recognizably worthy and aristocratic styles of life find expression in its vocational ideals.

In modern societies, of course, the variety of vocational ideals has been expanded. In many respects, the range of vocational ideals has also been democratized and "flattened." In societies like our own, for example, the moral and religious overtones of vocational ideals have been extensively relativized. Where previously persons were admired as vocational models because of their virtues and usefulness to society, now admiration is drawn to the appearances of success and wealth, to fascination with exciting and fast-moving lives, and to the name-face recognition that comes with public notoriety. Hence in our society we now claim the vocational models of the rock star, the movie celebrity, the sports idol, the eccentric millionaire-adventurer, and the television preacher-mogul.

Concurrent with this development, we have seen the erosion of the traditional professions as examples of vocational ideals. Increasingly, members of the traditional professions—medicine, law, religion, education, government, and public service—are being regarded predominantly as self-interested and opportunistic entrepreneurs. We all know and can mention by name persons who are exceptions to these generalizations and who serve, for those who know them, as representatives of their profession, restoring the respected quality of a vocational ideal. But the generalizations, more and more, have come to typify the expectations and estimates of the professions taken as a whole.

If the foregoing analysis makes sense, it means that we are in, or are moving toward, a crisis point with respect to vocational ideals in our society. Could it be that one major cluster of reasons for our crisis in public education has to do with our fundamental confusion over vocational ideals?

2. IMAGES OF GOOD MAN/GOOD WOMAN IN FERMENT

To suggest that we are experiencing a societal crisis of vocational ideals is to say that our normative images of what it means to be a good woman or a good man are in considerable ferment. The meaning of *adulthood* and the identification of worthy models for envisioning it, have become problematic for us. Many factors in our recent history and experience as a society help to account for this fermentative situation. Let me suggest a few.

The first set of factors contributing to altered perceptions and visions of worthy adulthood have to do with some fundamental changes in *demographics*. Some time ago I was reminded that at the turn of the century the average life expectancy for males in our society was age forty seven. For women, even then, it was slightly higher—fifty. Tied to that statistic was another that caught my attention. In 1900 there were as many single-parent households in our society, per capita, as there are today. But the reasons were quite different. Instead of separation and divorce, the reason most frequently was the death of one of the spouses.[2] When I read these statistics, I remembered my walks in the nineteenth-century graveyards of abandoned mountain churches in North Carolina, where I noted how many infants died before age two, how many women died in their early twenties, and how many men died before reaching forty.

Two related but distinct effects result from our expectations of greater longevity. On the one hand, we have the illusion, supported by statistical averages, that life is somehow less precarious than in other centuries and that we are entitled to, if not guaranteed, the biblical "three-score years and ten." With this, we assume as our right (at least if we consider ourselves in the upper-middle or upper class) access to the medical and nutritional resources that can support a full life-span. This mood, on the other hand, leads to a decided shift in the direction of "this-worldly" criteria for evaluating the well-lived life. It is difficult to know to what degree the hope of eternal life or personal immortality has declined as a source of courage and a motive for ethical and religious seriousness. It does seem certain, however, that the twentieth century has brought for most Americans the assumption of a long and full life span. This, in turn, has modified, both personally and culturally, the sense of time and timing in the "seasons" of our lives. It has also shifted powerfully the horizons of value and possibility in relation to which we determine the qualities of a good or well-lived life.

A second major cluster of factors contributing to ferment regarding our cultural images of the good man/good woman centers around mobility in our society. Physical mobility has, of course, characterized this nation of ex-immigrants from the beginning of our colonial and national life. But factors emerging with unique force since the 1930s have made us one of the most mobile societies in the world. The economic crises of the Depression era, coupled with automobiles and highways, led to vast displacements and movements of families and individuals seeking economic opportunity or survival. World War II, and the role of this nation in postwar world geopolitical leadership, moved American GIs, and often their families, to stations and residences in areas previously visited only by an elite group of monied and leisured Americans.

Corporate expansiveness and opportunities to move up the ladder of corporate success and power motivated American families to move frequently from state to state. The consolidation of small farms, the decline of livelihood for tenant farmers and sharecroppers, and the opportunities of assembly-line employment resulted in the large-scale migration of both black and white dwellers from the rural South to the inner cities of the North and Northeast. In all this, we experienced a steady growth in population, the development of transient suburban life, and the decline of stable small-town and rural-village culture.

Added to all we have said about physical mobility, there has been a widespread experience of social and economic mobility. An expanding economy, combined with widened opportunities and government support for higher education, has made it possible for many persons and families to realize the "American dream" by moving into the middle and upper-middle classes. And though they have achieved it with inflated dollars, there has been a noticeable democratization of the status "millionaire," resulting in a swelling of the ranks of what constitutes a new economic upper class.

All of these factors of physical and social mobility correlate with the relativization, if not breakdown, of traditional regional and small-town vocational ideals. They also represent the disruption of systems of interaction that formed and maintained societal consensus regarding worthy life-styles and aspirations. In the loneliness of suburban life, in the *anomie* of condominium society, and in the transient relations of the changing corporate workplace, it now requires an extraordinary kind of intentionality and investment of energy to form and maintain a "moral community" of recognition and support for shared values and vocational ideals.

We touched on education as a contributor to recent social and economic mobility. I think we need to examine education, in its own right, as an umbrella term for a substantial set of factors that have contributed to confusion and the ferment of new possibilities in American life. While we may find the overall quality of public education and its results discouraging, we need to keep in mind the extraordinary vision and goals we have pursued as a society in trying to offer universal literacy and access to higher education for an entire population.[3] In these aspirations and goals, we are almost unique among the national societies of the world.

Since the early fifties, the percentage of high school graduates in our population has more than doubled. The numbers of those undertaking some form of education beyond high school has increased remarkably.[4] The emergence on a widespread basis of community junior colleges and technical schools has provided economically feasible access to higher education for many who otherwise would not have had it. As part of this development, community colleges and the evening programs of other colleges and universities have opened up "holding environments" in which persons can reflectively explore new options of life-style and work orientations. Such holding environments provide space for the assessment of one's life, for exposure to new options or models for living, and for gaining some support for the arduous and costly work of making changes in oneself.[5] Further, private and public universities and colleges have been forced to provide access to their regular degree programs for men and women from minority and underprivileged economic groups, thus opening new avenues of entry into professional and managerial ranks.

New general levels and norms of education have subtle but pervasive and important impacts on how people at large think about what constitutes quality and worthiness in their lives.[6] These changes create the need for and an ability to use perspectives that can provide them with reflective handles on their experience. These changes encourage persons to examine the images of man/womanhood they have inherited, or absorbed through the media, and to make more critically self-aware choices.

We have already anticipated another decisive emergence that contributes to our present sense of ferment regarding norms for worthy adulthood: the unavoidable recognition of a rich and highly diverse *pluralism* in our society. When I first began to be aware of these kinds of issues in the 1950s, sociologists and historians had taught us to think of our national life with the image of the "melting pot."[7] The second generation of the children of immigrant parents would, we were told, do all that they could to shuck the marks of their immigrant origins and to discard the distinctive features linking them to the lands of their parents. They would leave the language, religious patterns, and styles of dress—as well as the ghetto communities—of their parents and exert every effort to become all-American citizens. Will Herberg, who was among my teachers at Drew University in the mid-sixties, wrote a book in that period called *Protestant, Catholic, Jew*.[8] Herberg's major thesis argued that the great religious divisions suggested by his book's title were, by the 1950s, but three relatively indistinguishable avenues for participation in the real religious patterns of most Americans, a kind of lowest-common-denominator version of a civil religion that we designated as "the American way of life."

The prophecies of the melting pot, as we all know, did not prove to be very lasting. In the sixties and beyond, we began to see people reclaiming their ethnic, racial, cultural, and religious particularities. Michael Novak wrote a book called *The Rise of the Unmeltable Ethnics*[9] and he, with others, began to help us understand what a violent and wrenching image the idea of the melting pot had been. The election of John F. Kennedy to the presidency in 1960 can be seen as the symbolic end of the domination of American society by a secularized Protestant culture that had, in fact, been seriously eroding for more than thirty years.

The entry into American society of significant numbers of Vietnamese, Cambodians, and Chinese since the end of the war in Vietnam has greatly heightened the visible and real pluralism of our society. Add to this the inflow of Haitians, Cubans, Mexicans, and Middle-Easterners and we begin to appreciate the range of often-conflicting images of normative adulthood our culture is trying to integrate. In addition to the physical presence of representatives from many national and linguistic cultures, increased travel by college students, business people, and tourists has served to widen our experience of the relativity of our life-styles and values. Moreover, satellite telecommunication has forced large segments of our population into awareness of global events and movements and, to some degree of awareness, of the values and world views of such diverse groups as the Druse Muslims and El Salvadorian Christian revolutionaries.

Any Marxist account of the background of change, which has given rise to ferment and confusion regarding normative images of adulthood in our society, would begin with economic developments in this nation since World War II. Until 1980, at least, most Americans have believed that their real income has steadily increased. The presence in their homes of impressive arrays of consumer products constitutes convincing proof that their standards of living have been on the rise. Home ownership, until recently, has been relatively easy to get into and has provided tax advantages as well as a means of keeping pace with an otherwise distressing tide of continuing inflation. There has been a great deal of talk about increased leisure and discretionary time, in which growingly prosperous Americans could pursue activities of self-enjoyment and self-enhancement.

Daniel Yankelovich, in his 1981 book *New Rules: Searching for Self-Fulfillment in a World Turned Upside Down,*[10] documented what he has called the shift from an "ethic of self-denial," which characterized this society through World War II, to an "ethic of self-fulfillment," which has become dominant since the fifties. It was as though a culture and society that had been bound for many decades in a stance of self-denial and the passionate investment of its energies in coping with national emergencies could begin to pursue its postponed agenda. Having come through the stress of the Depression era, and having mobilized in unprecedented and heroic ways to lead in the defeat of truly world-threatening enemies in World War II, it was as though a whole people began to find the space, time, and the means to get on with the tasks of marrying, establishing families, continuing or completing education, and pursuing life's satisfactions and happiness. In the course of those pursuits, people began to come to terms with all that was new and changing in the postwar affluence of American society. And as a people, we began to come to terms with a long-postponed encounter with the tasks and challenges of our changed and changing inner lives.

When we reflect on the flood of techniques for self-examination and growth that became widely available to Americans in the sixties and seventies, we recognize that there must have been a deep and pervasive societal readiness for new dimensions of intimacy. Sensitivity groups, therapy groups, encounter groups, and a variety of other techniques spawned by humanistic psychology created a new ethos of introspection, instant self-disclosure, and the sharing of self. The spoken and unspoken promise underlying marathons and intensive group experiences was that of transformation: new dimensions of self-discovery, new depths of relation to others in honesty and sensitivity, new richness for lives capsulated in routine and jaded by conventional values and life-styles. During this same period, due to the increased availability of third-party payments for psychiatric services by health insurance programs, access to many forms of personal therapy was opened for middle-class America. In addition, theological seminaries, in cooperation with the burgeoning field of clinical pastoral education, built pastoral counseling into their curricula as a central focus. This not only contributed to the development of a new specialization in ministry; it also opened, through churches and pastoral counseling centers, new contexts for personal growth and change, blessed with religious sanction. Through courses in organizational and personnel development, businesses and industry widely appropriated and taught the new techniques—and value systems—of what we came to call the "human potential movement."

Traditional images of manhood/womanhood experienced "disestablishment" in the contexts of sensitivity and encounter groups. In the interest of spontaneity and the discovery of one's true self and in order to learn to recognize and claim one's "needs" —as the cliche goes, "to get my needs met"—people were led to loosen their hold on images of the self fashioned after the traditional models and roles. Experiences designed to alter people's relations to their bodies and to widen the range of their emotional and intuitional responses to self and others sanctioned a frankly open and experimental approach to sexuality and to issues of commitment and life-style.

As we enumerate factors contributing to our contemporary experience of ferment regarding vocational ideals and cultural images of good manhood/womanhood, we have to include the waves of liberation movements that have eroded the beaches of traditional sexual, racial, political, and religious relations. Taken individually and taken as a whole, the movements toward inclusion and justice for blacks and other minority groups, for women, for gays and lesbians, and for third-world revolutionaries, have fundamentally altered and enriched this culture's previous consensual images of beauty, excellence, and the virtues of good manhood/womanhood.

Finally, I must say something, in a preliminary way, about the changed and changing role of religious authority with respect to the definitive images of vocational ideals. The interplay of all the factors I have enumerated in this brief historical and sociological discussion is extraordinarily complex. Nowhere is that complexity more in evidence than in the area of religion. Perhaps the most visible and useful symbol of change and ferment in religious authority in the post–World War period is the Second Vatican Council. Protestants and Jews have experienced their own equivalent transformations, but they have been less publicly visible because they have been more institutionally fragmented. But with Vatican II we beheld the spectacle—truly remarkable—of an international communion of faith, solemnly and publicly going through the anguish of fundamentally altering its self-definition and its structures of authority. From a church defined by the hierarchy and its authoritative control of tradition and scripture, we saw a move to a church defined as the "people of God." Within limits that are still being fought over, "the people of God" were given access to scripture and tradition and called to personal responsibility, with the hierarchy, for shaping faithful lives and institutions in an acknowledged pluralistic world. Confusing to many Catholics, liberating and exhilarating to many others, the normative images of Christian adulthood fostered by the church themselves became more pluralistic. Individual Catholics and local congregations were freed—and burdened—to take responsibility for implementing the guidelines of significantly reworked doctrinal and social-ethical teachings of the church. As one traditional Catholic lay person put it, "If the Church can change the rules about eating meat on Fridays and about saying the mass in Latin, what *can't* be changed?" Many devout Catholic families find that, intergenerationally, they are loyal to two different churches—one pre–Vatican II, the other post–Vatican II.

I have used the Catholic instance to illustrate a broader movement among churches and synagogues. A significant number of adherents in all these communities have claimed personal responsibility for appropriating the traditions of which they are a part and have taken authority to integrate religious teachings into their lives on the basis of their own judgments and experiences. This approach has inevitably altered the role of clergy and theologians as authorities; it has opened the way for struggles over religiously normative images of the virtues and character of good manhood/womanhood.

3. FROM "IDEOLOGICAL TEPEE" TO PROTEUS: CONTINUITY AND CHANGE

The interlocking range of factors I have discussed in the previous section, plus many more that I have not described, help to explain a fundamental shift that has occurred in this culture's images of adulthood in the past thirty years. Many of us over forty can remember childhoods in stable environments—whether urban, rural, or small town—where adulthood appeared and was experienced as a fairly static condition. Some years ago my mentor and friend, Carlyle Marney, offered a graphic image of this older, more static image of adulthood. He called it the "tepee model" of adulthood.[11]

When you build a tepee, you fix a number of poles in a circular pattern. You incline them together to a point. You bind the poles together firmly at the top, and then you stretch skins or canvas tightly over the frame. The tent poles, in this analogy, represent a set of ideological commitments or assumptions that one had to assemble in the process of becoming an adult. By the time one was in the late teens or early twenties, it was assumed that he/she would be settling a number of matters regarding values and life-style: One would put in place a pole dealing with choices of work or occupation. One would establish a pole in relation to marriage and location of residence. The meaning of regional identifications would be embraced and constitute an ideological tent pole—the meaning and loyalties deriving from roots in east Texas or western North Carolina, or from being a "down-East Yankee" or a "Hoosier." Another pole would consist of sex-role identifications: clear values and images of what it meant to be a woman or a man, and the range of acceptable gender roles and relations. Other poles in the tepee derived from economic and political values and iden-tifications. Typically there would be a religious pole, made visible by membership and identification with a church or temple. There would also be a pole or poles deriving from racial and ethnic iden-tifications and their accompanying social meanings.

When the young adult had assembled these ideological tent poles, Marney suggested, he/she could bind them together in an often tacit or unexamined unity. Then a covering could be stretched over the structure, and the young man or woman could enter this ideological hut to dwell and never have to come out again.

In this older, more static image of adulthood, it was expected that the essential structure would be in place by the mid to late twenties. If one reached thirty without having built it, people would say, "He has not found himself" (implying that the "self" is analogous to a Platonic ideal form, waiting somewhere in the darkness to be found and embraced). Or if in the late thirties or forties the ideological tepee should begin to be buffeted by the changes and struggles of life—the tent poles rattling, the cover flapping—people would say, "She seems to be having a nervous breakdown." Character, in this view of adulthood, meant consis-tency, predictability, and stability of values, attitudes, commit-ments, and life-style. Often it also meant the expectation of con-tinuity of residence and relationships in the same town or area.

Of course, the tepee model is a caricature, too extreme in its depiction of an older, more static image of adulthood. But as an image it may prove helpful for us in the effort to grasp and characterize our present situation of ferment regarding normative images of adulthood. Let me invite you to consider another caricature of a style of adulthood, this time from the opposite end of a continuum of stability and change.

Robert Jay Lifton, a Yale psychiatrist, has pioneered the study of psychohistory, which he defines as inquiry into the relations between large-scale historical change and individual patterns of adaptation. Among other interests, Lifton has studied the survivors of catastrophic disasters. He coined the now-familiar term *survival guilt* to describe a complex of feelings characteristic of those who have the burden of making sense of terrible events in which friends, loved ones, and others were obliterated, while they themselves were spared. Lifton, who has conducted much of his research in the Far East, spent considerable time in Japan in the early sixties. There he devoted many hours to interviewing young adults who as children were survivors of the atomic bombing of Hiroshima and Nagasaki.

As Lifton analyzed the stories of these young adult survivors in Japan, he began to note a pattern of commitment and change in their lives that arrested him. Again and again he saw that in their teens and early adulthood they seemed to have rapidly made, and then changed, a series of fundamental relational and ideological commitments. He was surprised by the intensity of their commitments and then by their frequent withdrawals and turns, often in diametrically opposed directions. As Lifton pursued other research with survivors—victims of Chinese "brainwashing" or thought-control experiments who escaped to Hong Kong—and with American students in the turbulence of the sixties in this country, he began to see that this pattern could be generalized. In order to link this pattern with a name and an image, Lifton reached into Greek mythology. Proteus was a minor god in the court of Poseidon, the god of the sea. "Proteus," said Lifton, "was able to change his shape with relative ease—from wild boar to lion to dragon to fire to flood. But what he did find difficult, and would not do unless seized and chained, was to commit himself to a single form, a form most his own, and carry out his function of prophecy."[12]

For a time in the sixties, some social commentators—and to some degree, Lifton himself—suggested that perhaps Protean man held together the elements of an adaptive way of responding to an era of unrelenting change. In that view, it was virtuous to be fluid, flexible, and frequently ready to change fundamental convictions and outlooks. Lifton felt that two major historical factors helped account for the emergence of the Protean pattern:

The first is the worldwide sense of . . . *historical* (or *psychohistorical*) *dislocation,* the break in the sense of connection which men have long felt with the vital and nourishing symbols of their cultural tradition—symbols revolving around family, idea-systems, religions, and the life-cycle in general . . . . The second large historical tendency is the *flooding of imagery* produced by the extraordinary flow of post-modern cultural influences over mass-communication networks. These . . . cause (contemporary persons) to be overwhelmed by superficial messages and undigested cultural elements, by headlines and by endless partial alternatives in every sphere of life."[13]

Like the image of the ideological tepee, the Protean person, as a type, is a caricature. But perhaps the two caricatures, taken as extremes on a continuum, will serve to represent something of the shift, within the lifetime of many of us, from a largely stable, not to say static, image of adulthood to one that, in its extreme forms, manifests great fluidity and instability. I believe that the tepee and the Protean models depict, in polar tension, two yearnings and realities that pull powerfully at one another in the hearts of each of us and in the culture of which we are a part. These yearnings and realities—the experience of relentless change and the longing for continuity and stability—persist and conflict in the midst of the shifting tectonic plates of values and convictions underlying our societal and cultural life.

One of the principal reasons for the present widespread acceptance and embrace of psychological theories of adult development, I believe, is that they provide us with narrative frameworks for holding together our profound expriences—and tensions—of change and continuity. In this and in other ways that I shall consider with you now, they are providing normative and descriptive images of adulthood that uniquely and powerfully speak to the situation of cultural ferment and the confusion of vocational ideals in our society.

4. ADULT DEVELOPMENTAL THEORISTS AS PHILOSOPHERS AND GOSSIPS

Theorists of adult development have begun to play the role in our society that storytellers and mythmakers once played in primitive and classical cultures. They have taken on many of the functions that philosophers and theologians performed in the twelfth through the nineteenth centuries. In our time of fractured images of the human vocation and of fragmented experiences of connectedness to religious and cultural symbols of wholeness, a group of philosophical psychologists are helping us to gain a holistic grasp on the course of human life. Using the organic root metaphor of development in a variety of ways, their research and theories aim to provide empirically grounded chartings of predictable patterns and turnings in human life cycles. Seventeenth-century Protestant scholastic theologians wrote and taught about what they called the *ordo salutis*—the path or steps to salvation. It may not be going too far to suggest that philosophical theorists of developmental psychology are offering, in formalistic and mainly secular terms, contemporary versions of an *ordo salutis*. This parallel makes more sense if you recall that in Latin *salus,* the root word for *salutis* and *salvation,* means "wholeness" or "completion."

Consider these further contributions of philosophical adult developmental psychologies: They name and map our experiences of personal change, providing reassurance that many of the crises we experience can be understood in developmental terms. They help us reduce our reliance on classifications and diagnostic terminology derived from the study of pathology. They enable us to see that much of our dis-ease can be understood as "sickness unto new health"—a developmental transition—rather than as a "sickness unto death." Providing a language for our experiences of change, they also offer normative depictions of the *telos* or goals of human life. Their theories provide benchmarks or blazes by which we can determine where we are on the human life course. They provide guidance and encouragement regarding the direction and challenges of the next step.

In the next two chapters of this book, I will invite you to examine with me the perspectives of four philosophical theories of adult development. In Chapter II, the theories of Erik Erikson, Daniel Levinson, and Carol Gilligan will receive our attention. In Chapter III, I shall try to deal in a similar way with the theory of faith development for which I and my associates have been the principal researchers. While we shall give attention to the research and empirical foundations of these theories, our principal interest, for purposes of this book, will focus elsewhere. Our main concern will be to clarify the theories' images of the human being struggling toward psychological and ethical maturity—their images of the course of the human movement toward wholeness and completion. We shall treat these developmental theories as narrative structures, as myths of becoming, that elaborate both the quality and the direction of human growth and development.

If I have not overstated the case for regarding philosophical developmental psychologies as contemporary myths and philosophical statements, they deserve both our attention and our critical evaluation. Our evaluation must focus on their claims to descriptive adequacy—their claims to be the results of scientific research. But equally important, and more so for this particular project, we must engage these myths of becoming with ethical and theological criteria of adequacy. We must treat their theorists as quasi-ethicists and quasi-theologians.

But why have I referred to adult developmental theorists, including myself, as gossips? This kind of reference began as a humorous recognition of the fact that part of what makes these writings attractive to wide audiences is their interesting and extensive use of case materials from their research. Jokingly, I made reference to the fact that in our transient contemporary life we miss the leisure and the small-town continuities of relationship with neighbors that made gossip not only a form of dubious entertainment but also an important source of life wisdom. But one day when I decided to look up the derivation of the word *gossip* in the *Oxford English Dictionary*, I found reason to take my reference to adult developmental theorists as gossips more seriously. *Gossip* derives from the two roots *god* and *sib,* the latter meaning "akin" or "related." Put together, they meant "one who has contracted spiritual affinity with another by acting as a sponsor at baptism." Hence a gossip could be a godfather or a godmother or a fellow sponsor of one who is to be baptized. From this rather surprising sixteenth-century understanding of gossip, the term degenerated to today's common usage: "a person, mostly a woman, of light and trifling character, especially one who delights in idle talk; a rumormonger, a tattler." One final use of gossip refers to it as a product: "easy, unrestrained talk or writing, especially about persons or social incidents."[14]

To refer to adult developmental theorists as gossips is to reclaim the original notion of one who has contracted to serve as sponsor in a critical rite of passage. It is to suggest that the narrative frameworks of developmental theories provide support and clarification for the passages of our lives. It is also to acknowledge that we do learn a great deal about life from the opportunity to look deeply into the lives-in-progress of our contemporaries or forebears. The disciplined manner of investigating and reporting their findings maximizes the possibility that the study of lives can yield wisdom. Moreover, the methods of research employed by adult developmental theorists, involving lengthy interviews and relationships of co-inquiry with their subjects, provide unique and humane modes of access to sources of insight for living our lives.

NOTES

1. *The Westminster Shorter Catechism* 2nd ed., with analysis, scriptural proofs, explanatory and practical inferences, and illustrative anecdotes by James R. Boyd. (New York: M. W. Dodd, 1856).
2. See Arlene Skolnick and Jerome Skolnick eds., *Intimacy, Family and Society* (Boston: Little, Brown and Company, 1974), 15–16; and Tamara K. Harevan, "Family Time and Historical Time," *Daedalus,* Vol. 106, No. 2, (Spring 1977): pp. 62–63.
3. A representative statement of alarm about decline in educational quality in this country can be found in *A Nation at Risk: The Imperative for Educational Reform,* a report of The National Commission on Excellence in Education (Washington, D.C., April 1983). For an impressive account of the informing visions and institutional developments of education in this country see Lawrence A. Cremin's magisterial two-volume study *American Education* (New York: Harper & Row, 1970–80).
4. In 1950 33.4% of the U.S. population reported that they had completed four or more years of high school. In 1983 71% made the same claim, according to the *Digest of Educational Statistics,* United States Department of Education, (Washington, D.C., 1983–84). According to the *World Almanac and Book of Facts* (Newspaper Enterprise Association, Inc., New York, 1984), the percentage of persons claiming one to three years of college increased from 11.75 to 24.2% between 1950 and 1982 (See table, page 194).
5. The term "holding environment" comes from child-psychiatrist D. W. Winnicott. My use of the term here, however, has been most influenced by Robert G. Kegan's *The Evolving Self.* (Cambridge: Harvard University Press, 1981).
6. A variety of developments in communications make it difficult to generalize, as was frequently done in the sixties, about the level of cognitive development assumed to characterize the reading and listening public. Radio stations and programs have become particularly sophisticated in targeting their audiences with regard to interests, educational levels, and affluence. Newspapers and television must still reach broader and less differentiated audiences, but the highly sophisticated studies of audiences and ratings which television networks employ are rapidly being matched by similar research on readers of different genres of newspaper materials.
7. Nathan Glazer and Daniel Patrick Moynihan trace the image of America as the "melting pot" back to the beginnings of the Republic. A play by Jewish immigrant Israel Zangwill appeared in 1908 with the title "The Melting Pot." One of the characters in the play, a new immigrant, says: "America is God's Crucible, the great Melting Pot where all the races of Europe are melting and reforming! . . . A fig for your feuds and vendettas! German and Frenchman, Irishman and Englishman, Jews and Russians—into the Crucible with you all! God is making the American." Quoted in Nathan Glazer and Daniel Patrick Moynihan, *Beyond the Melting Pot* (Cambridge: MIT Press and Harvard University Press), 1963, p. 289.
8. Will Herberg, *Protestant, Catholic, Jew: An Essay in American Religious Sociology* (Garden City, New York: Doubleday, 1955).

9. Michael Novak, *The Rise of the Unmeltable Ethnics: Politics and Culture in the Seventies* (New York: Macmillan, 1972).

10. Daniel Yankelovich, *New Rules: Searching for Self-Fulfillment in a World Turned Upside Down* (New York: Random House, 1981).

11. I heard Marney use this metaphor in oral presentations at Interpreters' House, Lake Junaluska, N.C., in 1968–69. I have not found references to it in his writings. For a biography of Marney see John J. Carey, *Carlyle Marney: A Pilgrim's Progress* (Macon: Mercer University Press, 1980).

12. Robert Jay Lifton, *History and Human Survival* (New York: Vintage Books, 1971), p. 319.

13. Ibid., p. 318.

14. *The Compact Edition of the Oxford English Dictionary* (New York: Oxford University Press, 1971), Vol. I, p. 1179.

II. Developmentalists as Philosophers and Gossips

1. ERIK H. ERIKSON: TOWARD GENERATIVE ADULTHOOD

The language and concepts of adult developmental theories have invaded our everyday talk. Often our use of terms such as *identity, intimacy, mid-life crisis,* or *individuation* fail to take account of their origins and place in elaborated theories of the life cycle. My point in undertaking this and the subsequent discussions of contemporary philosophical psychologists is to try, economically, to show the full sweep of their developmental perspectives on human living. I do this, not so much to reiterate what they have said in detail about "stages" and "transitions," but rather to focus what they have to teach us about human destiny and wholeness. I want to help readers see the visions of human maturity that animate the works of Erik Erikson, Daniel Levinson, and Carol Gilligan. The most revealing aspect of any theory of human development is the character of the last stages. What vision of completion, of fullness of being, of maturity informs the research on and definitions of stages or phases of development?

It is as ethicists and philosophers, therefore, that I propose to approach Erikson, Levinson, and Gilligan. Such expositions of ages and phases as I offer here will be incidental to our effort to clarify their visions of the good man and the good woman.

Since 1950, when he published *Childhood and Society,*[1] Erik Erikson has assumed something of the role of a guru in our society. For students in college classes in personality theory and for graduate students in psychiatry, social work, and theology, Erikson's familiar "Eight Ages of the Life Cycle" have opened ways toward fruitful understandings of self and others. Erikson is, of course, a pioneer in the study of the life cycle. He has worked as a child psychoanalyst and has written insightfully about childhood. (He was an early analysand of Anna Freud. She had selected him to work with her in child psychoanalysis because of his training as a Montessori teacher. As well, he impressed her with the creative use of his artistic background in his work with children at a small school for the children of Sigmund Freud's English-speaking patients.) Soon after he moved to the United States, he participated in an anthropological study of childrearing practices and social institutions in two American Indian tribes. Later Erikson worked as a researcher and therapist with troubled adolescents, from both privileged homes and the homes of steelworkers and tenant farmers. In the latter years of his career, Erikson has combined continuing work as a therapist to adolescents and adults with his growing absorption as a writer and teacher. In his writings he has helped to lay the foundations for the new interdisciplinary field of psychohistory, in which he has contributed studies of the young Martin Luther, Thomas Jefferson, Mahatma Gandhi, and others.[2]

A growing theme and focus in Erikson's work has been his concern with the ethical dimensions of human growth and human societies. He has consistently concerned himself with the study of the "growth and crises of the healthy personality."[3] He has combined this interest with a parallel concern for studying how societies can and do make provisions, through practices of childrearing, family life, and institutional arrangements, for supporting growing persons in the development of the kinds of strengths that are essential for both moral and nonmoral virtue.

Erikson sees the ages and phases of the life cycle in terms of what he calls an "epigenetic" schedule of emerging capacities and challenges. The maturation of the body on schedule correlates with challenges to mental and emotional development. At the same time, the growing person is both supported by and required to take on new roles and responsibilities by social groups and institutions. Erikson's work as a therapist and his observations as a researcher in this and other societies has led him to see a sequence of emergent challenges and crises that the developing ego must meet. *(Ego,* for Erikson, refers to the largely unconscious psychic activities of adaptation, synthesis, and the shaping of meanings that underlie emotional and personality growth.) Reminding us that *crisis* refers to a "turning point," Erikson has helped us see that the emergent crises of personality development in fact represent times at which the overall strength of one's personhood is at stake. Each ascendant crisis holds potentials for new dimensions of ego strength or virtue. At the same time, each ascendant crisis also holds the possibility of an overall weakening of personhood.

Let us consider briefly Erikson's schedule of the crises of the life cycle, with their dangers and their possibilities of contributing to a person's strength.[4] First there is, of course, infancy. Here the basic crisis with which the infant and its primary relational environment must deal has to do with the formation of a consistent disposition of trust, in opposition to the constant undertow of anxiety and basic mistrust. Both trust and mistrust in this earliest phase have to do with self, others, and environment. Even though there is not yet a clearly developed sense of self, it does make sense to speak of a "disposition"—a deep and consistent feeling about the world one is brought into, about the people who constitute it and provide welcome, and about that center of all feeling and processing that the infant is beginning slowly to recognize as self. When care and consistency and the organic "animal faith" of the baby win a favorable balance of trust over the never-banished presence of basic mistrust, the virtue—the ego strength—of *hope* is the lasting gift the growing child carries to the next and subsequent stages.

At or around two Erikson has taught us to see the childish ego struggling for some months with the emergent crisis of autonomy versus the threats of shame and (self) doubt. Here the issues that dominate the child's emotional and mental growth have to do with the process of differentiation from primal others. Literally and figuratively, the toddler is learning to "stand on her own two feet." She is also newly aware of vulnerability and dependence, and—in a first kind of self-consciousness—is mindful of being seen. Shame is a feeling of being exposed when one fears being found deficient. Doubt is an organic sense that one can and never will "measure up." At stake in this drama of the two-year-old's stepping onstage is the growing person's capacity for claiming "space" and for requiring that others acknowledge her presence and honor her claims to attention and regard. A favorable balance on the side of autonomy manifests itself in the child's movements, as in the later adult's capacity for assertion, through the virtue or strength of *will*.

The ascendant crisis of the older preschool child Erikson finds focused around the development of conscience. In a complex process of internalization, the child, beginning to prepare for life beyond the confines of the family, makes the expectations and the ideal aspirations held by a parent or parents (and other primally important persons, frequently grandparents) a commanding part of her own system of guidance and self-evaluation. When these aspirations are offered too compellingly as conditions of worth, or when the parent(s)' expectations and performance don't match, the child may overconstrict herself in the effort to meet conditions that are impossible to fulfill for membership in the family unit. Erikson long ago described this crisis as the struggle of initiative versus guilt. A favorable balance toward initiative empowers a child to trust her *own* aspirations and desires, and to balance them with the requirements and aspirations for her of those whom she loves. Competition and struggle can be undertaken without paralyzing self-recriminations. Erikson identifies the strength this attainment represents and offers to subsequent development as the virtue of *purpose*.

The contribution that the crisis of the school years makes to the overall strength of personhood arises out of the struggle of industry with feelings and experiences of inferiority. Schooling, and its equivalent in every society, is the social institution—formal or informal—in which care is taken to help the young learn the skills, disciplines, and patterns of social cooperation that will enable them to be effective actors, later as adults, in the dramas of societal maintenance and renewal. Sometimes this work is done badly by a society. Sometimes a child's preschool experience is such that he is ill-prepared for school life, emotionally or otherwise. Sometimes moves, family crises, or other disruptions prevent the stability required for the development of skills and the appropriation of the social confirmation that such development brings. When such failures occur, the child is frequently left with a residue of felt inferiority. When this enterprise works, added to the previous virtues of hope, will, and purpose there will emerge the strength of *competence*—the portable confidence that not only has one learned but that one now has learned *how* to learn in situations requiring innovation and change.

Adolescence seems to have held a particular fascination for Erikson. In one of his autobiographical writings, he alludes to the fact that his own adolescence was a particularly troubled time in his life. He reports painful experiences of feeling that he didn't belong anywhere in his youth. He says that in the city of Karlsruhe, Germany, where he lived in the home of his stepfather, Dr. Homburger, he was considered a Jew by antisemitic gentiles. In his stepfather's synagogue, his blue eyes and Nordic features earned him the label "goy." To German-speaking nationalists, his accent made him a Dane. Erikson expresses lasting gratitude to his stepfather, however, for his support of a year or two of what the Germans call "Wanderjahre," a time of traveling on one's own or with friends, often walking long distances (in those times), and reading and discussing art, literature, and politics. His own experience of wandering seems to have been healing for Erikson. We see his appreciation of that set of experiences in his coining the term *moratorium* to describe a time in a youth's life when premature overcommitment to a life direction can be avoided by a temporary but crucial period of time devoted to the search for values and a sustaining world view. Erikson describes the emergent crisis of adolescence as the struggle for identity, a struggle against the inability to construct an integral unity of one's gifts, potential roles, and images of the self, the condition that he calls "identity confusion." When, through the fidelity of some others and the finding of a cause or causes worthy of one's devotion, one begins to experience the unity and self-recognition of identity, then the person is ready to make commitments and exercise the emergent virtue of this stage, *fidelity*.

For his discussion of the central emotional crisis of young adulthood, Erikson has claimed the term *intimacy*. By that he means a readiness to risk the self in relations of closeness with that which is "other" or opposite. The prototype of intimacy is sexual love in the context of a committed relationship. Intimacy, by its very nature, requires an element of exclusiveness of commitment and sharing. But Erikson also sees intimacy as characterizing situations of conflict and struggle, situations of intellectual and spiritual communion, and situations where persons from differing religious or cultural orientations meet and share their traditions' truths deeply and unthreateningly. The opposite tendency to intimacy, which makes this dimension of young adulthood critical, is the danger of isolation. In isolation one must either control situations of potential intimacy, or one withdraws from them. A third, paradoxical failure of intimacy is fusion. With fusion there may be physical or spiritual closeness, but it is a closeness that dissolves boundaries and breaks down separateness (or prevents their development), thereby losing the essence of the kind of communion that constitutes true intimacy. The virtue or strength that emerges with a balance toward intimacy is that of *love*.

With the concepts of generativity versus stagnation Erikson characterizes the ascendant challenge that our adaptive and reintegrative capacities must address in middle adulthood. We will look more closely at this crisis, and the model of full adulthood it implies, in a few moments. In a major sense, stagnation, if it proves to be more than a transient series of moments in the passages of mid-life, means a condition of being emotionally curved in upon the self. In the language of Otto Kernberg, stagnation describes forms of the "unhealthy narcissism" of middle age. As Erikson puts it, one makes of oneself one's own favored child. In stagnation one tries, with pseudo-intimacy, to recoup relational deficits, but without genuine giving of the self or receiving of others. When generativity outweighs stagnation, persons' lives show the strength or virtue of *care,* about which we will say more shortly.

The emotional and developmental crisis of old age Erikson identifies as integrity versus despair. Integrity is the fruit of a life that has found a basis for self-acceptance and for confirming one's life as worthwhile. Integrity seems to come with the considered feeling that one played the roles and met the challenges of each of the eras of the life cycle. It does not mean perfection; it does not mean the absence of regrets. It does mean having found a way to make one's life count in caring for—and hopefully enhancing—the ongoing flow of life. From the experiences one gathers, from the suffering and the gladness, one accrues the virtue Erikson calls *wisdom.*

In this brief overview of Erikson's vision of the life cycle, I have accentuated the philosophical and ethical dimensions of his work. I have sought to lay the foundations for a summary statement in which we can pull together some of the main ideas Erikson offers regarding the construction of a contemporary vocational ideal. Our concern is to clarify Erikson's vision of the good man/good woman.

In the formulation of this summary, I am much indebted to the two chapters on Erikson included in Don Browning's book, *Generative Man.*[5] Browning first helped me see that Erikson's ethical vision, including his normative image of mature personhood, can only be grasped by seeing how each of the previous crises and their emergent virtues contribute to the cumulative integration of strengths that constitute adult generativity. A chart reproduced from Browning's book will help us get a schematic grasp of the point I am trying to make. (See Fig. 1, next page).

In summary, Erikson's model of the mature adult envisions a person who has reaped the fruits of the more or less successful negotiation of the crises of the epigenetic schedule, as follows:

1. This is the adult who has formed and re-formed a strong foundation of basic trust, expressed and grounded in a religious faith or a philosophical confidence that life has meaning.

Figure 1.   Developmental Interrelationships In Erikson

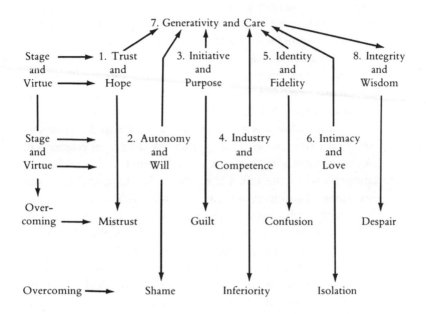

Source: Don S. Browning, Generative Man: Psychoanalytic Perspective (Philadelphia: Westminster Press, 1972), p. 182.

2. This is a person who has a sense of independence, an ability to stand alone, if necessary, on matters of principle. She has clear identity boundaries that make it possible to say a clear no or a clear yes, without undue coldness and distance, on the one hand, or an excessively compliant closeness, on the other.

3. The mature adult has a capacity for initiative and purpose, as well as for what the existentialists call "having a project." Having a mature conscience, based on examination and considered choice of values and principles, she has reworked the moralistic, harsh conscience of childhood.

4. The generative adult has a capacity for work and has devel-

oped a set of competencies that equip her to be a productive contributor to society and to carry effectively the roles and responsibilities these bring.

5. In the generative person, an adult sense of identity has taken form that can incorporate the range of personal relationships, roles, and aptitudes, as well as limits, into an integrated configuration. This means, to use Browning's phrase, "having a personally satisfying and publicly convincing answer to the question 'Who are you?' "[6]

6. The mature adult has a capacity for intimacy and a readiness based on a firm sense of identity to risk the self in relations of closeness to others, without a paralyzing fear of the loss or compromise of the self. He needs neither to withdraw from situations of intimacy, on the one hand, nor to dominate or destroy that which would get too close, on the other. Practically speaking, this means a readiness for sexual intimacy, with the ability to maintain the structure of exclusivity of love and commitment that such lasting intimacy entails (though as Erikson well recognizes, one may decide in principle for vocational reasons not to exercise such a capacity in physical ways). This capacity for intimacy carries over into readiness to engage in conflict without withdrawal or the need to destroy the opponent, and it sustains one in situations of shared inspiration and creation.

As the chart in Figure 1 suggests, Browning sees the quality of adult being that Erikson calls generativity as constituted by the culmination and integration of the virtues or strengths that persons generate in the course of ego development. *Generativity,* for Erikson, means creativity and productiveness, to be sure, but it also means much more. It means, deriving from the same root as *generation,* the adult person having found ways, through love and work, creativity and care, to contribute to the conditions that will provide the possibility for members of the oncoming generations to develop their personal strengths at each stage. The tragedy of persons who give into stagnation, in Erikson's view, is that in devoting their major care to the effort to remedy or reclaim what was lost or never gained in their own earlier lives, they lose their opportunity to be contributors, in their time, to the strengthening of the ongoing cycle of generations.

If you ask Erik Erikson, then, what it means to be a mature adult, he might answer in some such words as these:

To have found a way, by midlife and beyond, in our love and work and care to contribute to the maintenance of the strength of the human soul, and to extend the conditions in social life that will make it possible for the next generation to have optimal opportunity to develop their full measure of human strength.

Such persons, in Erikson's view, can face old age and oncoming death with a sense of integrity, which overcomes or offsets the grief and the fear of death. Though Erikson makes no appeal to belief in a life after death in this vision, he clearly affirms the importance, and even the necessity, of faith in the sustaining of lives of meaning and devotion.

Erikson plainly intends that his perspective on the development of human virtue and strength should be seen in correlation with a social ethic. Societies, he intends, should be critically assessed in terms of the provisions they make, through government, education, commerce, industry, and voluntary associations, for guaranteeing each member the full opportunity and support for developing the virtues of each stage of the life cycle. Erikson, in calling these strengths "virtues," sees the close interdependence between the capacities for moral virtue (justice, fairness, commitment to the common good, steadfastness, and loyalty) and these strengths of personhood.

The thought world of Erik Erikson pushes us in the direction of ethics and normative visions of human wholeness. Finally, I am suggesting, Erikson's vision is prophetic and religious in its clear suggestion that fulfillment in life derives from caring for the conditions that enable present and future generations to develop the full range of human virtues.

2. DANIEL J. LEVINSON: SEASONS AND WISDOM

When we turn to the thought world of Daniel Levinson, we breathe a different air. If Erikson's work has some affinity with the prophetic literature of the Bible, Levinson's approach breathes more the spirit of the wisdom literature. When I read *The Seasons of a Man's Life* by Levinson and his associates, I think of Ecclesiastes 3:1-8 (ASV):

> There is an appointed time for everything. And there is a
> time for every event under heaven—
> A time to give birth, and a time to die;
> A time to plant, and a time to uproot what is planted.
> A time to kill, and a time to heal;
> A time to tear down, and a time to build up.
> A time to weep, and a time to laugh;
> A time to mourn, and a time to dance.
> A time to throw stones, and a time to gather stones;
> A time to embrace, and a time to shun embracing.
> A time to search, and a time to give up as lost;
> A time to keep, and a time to throw away.
> A time to tear apart, and a time to sew together;
> A time to be silent, and a time to speak.
> A time to love, and a time to hate;
> A time for war, and a time for peace.

Levinson has carefully reflected on the derivation and images of the life cycle. Attend to what he has written regarding the two key elements he finds in the idea of life cycle: "First, there is the idea of a process or a journey from a starting point (birth or origin) to a termination point (death or conclusion)."[7] (I remember Erikson referring to his students' joking images of this movement from starting point to end point in his course on the life cycle at Harvard —'from womb to tomb," "from bust to dust," or "from sperm to germ," they said.) Levinson continues:

To speak of a general human life cycle is to propose that the journey from birth to old age follows an underlying universal pattern on which there are endless cultural and individual variations. Many influences along the way shape the nature of the journey, but as long as the journey continues, it follows the same basic sequence.

Second, there is the idea of *seasons:* a series of periods or stages within the life cycle. The process is not a simple, continuous flow. There are qualitatively different seasons, each having its own distinctive character. Every season is different from those that precede and follow it, though it also has much in common with them. The imagery of seasons takes many forms. There are seasons in the year: Spring is a time of blossoming, winter a time of death but also of rebirth and the start of a new cycle. There are seasons, too, within a single day—daybreak, noon, dusk, the quiet dark of night—each having its diurnal, atmospheric and psychological character. There are seasons in a love relationship, in war, politics, artistic creation and illness.[8]

Levinson and his team, based on their research so far, see our lives as divided into four broad seasons of roughly twenty years each. The first twenty or so years of life comprise childhood and adolescence. Early adulthood takes up roughly the second twenty-year span. The third double decade constitutes middle adulthood, and the fourth twenty years, plus or minus, make up late adulthood. Between each of these major seasons Levinson sees an overlapping transitional period of about five years. These are the times when we literally move from one season to another. As we come to these periods we are rather like the Roman god Janus, from whom the name of the month January is taken. Janus, you remember, had two faces: One turned toward the past, and the other turned toward the future. When we come to one of these five-year seasonal transition times, the face looking backward symbolizes our concern with bringing to a culmination and completion the work of the era that is coming to an end. The face looking forward represents our engagement with the tasks of putting the pieces in place for moving into the next season.

Levinson and his team have introduced an important new concept as the focal point of their research. He has called it "the individual life structure." Instead of following Erikson, who focuses upon the individual ego in its adaptive and creative work, Levinson has studied the evolving life structure. What does he mean by this term? Your *life structure,* or mine, at any given point in our lives, is the pattern of relationships, roles, and consistent points of our exchange with the world. It includes our love relationships, our family ties, and the friendship and acquaintance networks that sustain us. It includes our religious affiliations and involvements as well as our work and professional roles and societies. It includes the patterns of our leisure activities, our public life as citizens, and our private lives. It is made up of all the ways we engage the world, on the one hand, and suffer the world's engagement with us, on the other. As we move from one season of our lives to another, the life structure undergoes development and modification.

In Levinson's theory *time* and *being* are closely interrelated. The major shifts from one season to another are precipitated by the convergence of a number of time-related indicators. Our bodies, with their changes in maturation and aging, serve as biological time clocks. They give us gradual but unmistakable clues to the passage of time and its effects on our personages. The signs are all familiar: shifts in weight distribution; changes in metabolic rate, affecting the amounts and kinds of food we need to eat; alterations in hairlines and hair color; modifications in energy level and sleeping patterns; changes in the meaning of sexuality in our self-concepts; and many more. Then there are what Bernice Neugarten calls our "social time clocks."[9] These are the clues and indicators of maturation and change that come through the responses and expectations of the persons and institutions with which we interact. In part, our social time clocks are a matter of having to encounter our peer reference groups. Why is it that all the other members of our high school graduating classes always look older than we do? But we also tell our social time by the age and status of our colleagues—suddenly everyone in our workplace is our age or younger. We move from being promising young adults (both to ourselves and others) to being persons reasonably well defined in our particular patterns of gifts and limitations. People tell us how old they take us to be by their responses to us. One of the most interesting social clock adjustments for a professor comes in that era when his students are suddenly not much older than his own children and when the students make it clear, despite whatever illusions the professor may have of being an older member of their generation, that in their view he belongs with their parents.

Levinson's research, conducted originally with forty men, has now been expanded to include a sample of forty-five women. His fundamental insight and claim is that for men and women alike, the inner and outer clues to the aging process bring us periodically to the major seasonal times when our present life structures must be fundamentally re-examined, assessed, and modified. The chart in Figure 2, taken from *The Seasons of a Man's Life*, shows the twenty-year pattern, linked by the overlapping times of transition described earlier. Within each of these long seasons Levinson and his team identified three subordinate phases he calls "periods." The first is a structure-building period—a time in which a person is constructing the pattern of commitments and relationships that will carry her into and establish her in the new season. Then there comes a second period that is essentially a time of testing and modifying the newly emerged life structure (the "Age 30" and "Age 50" transitions on the chart). The season closes or culminates in a third period in which the person endeavors to bring to a completion the significant enterprises of that season of her life.

Other key Levinson concepts that are becoming part of our language of adult development include the "dream" and the "mentor." Levinson's notion of the dream refers to the formation in young adulthood of a vision of the self, projected into the future, that gives the young person the energy, the sense of destiny and direction, and the courage to move purposefully into the ambiguities and difficulties of adult life. In a later chapter on destiny and vocation, I shall return to the idea of the dream.

The terms *mentor* and *mentoring* are currently being widely used and misused. In Levinson's much more restrictive usage, the mentor is a person usually seven to twenty years older than the one being mentored. The mentor takes an active interest in the life and dream of the younger adult and develops with him or her a quality of love relationship that constitutes a special kind of friendship.

Figure 2.   Developmental Periods in Early and Middle Adulthood

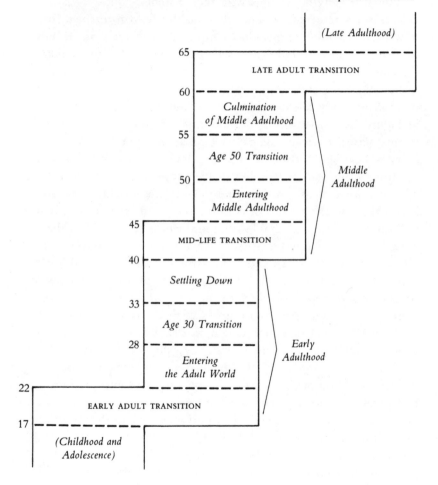

Source: Daniel J. Levinson et al., *The Seasons of a Man's Life* (New York: Knopf, 1978), p. 57.

The older partner in this special friendship grants to the younger a proleptic or anticipatory colleagueship. Generally this involves practical help in getting started or advancing in the field of interest they share, and it means a privileged relationship in which they engage in mutual teaching and sharing. This relationship represents an affirmation of the younger person's potential and identifies him or her as an outstanding and promising member of that generation. Successful mentoring relationships can continue for seven to ten years, or even longer. They end best when there is a mutual recognition that the younger person has, by dint of work and the achievement of competance, become a peer. Frequently, however, they end in a rupture caused by a mentor's continuing efforts to control the relation or in the rejecting assertion of a contested independence by the younger party.

In my judgment, we need to distinguish "mentoring," in this fairly restricted and exclusive sense, from what I prefer to call "sponsorship"—a less comprehensive and more short-term relationship. In sponsorship, one who is more experienced takes a generous and active hand in introducing another to an area, a skill, or a status.

Much more could be offered by way of exposition of Levinson's research and theory. By the time this book appears, I hope Levinson's current writing on the "seasons of women's lives" will be available. But our intention is to treat Levinson as we did Erikson —to ask what he has to contribute to our understanding of fulfilled human life. What does he offer us, in our appraisal of adult developmental psychologies, that can be seen as part of an emerging contemporary "vocational ideal"? What does he have to teach us about ethical images of the good man/good woman?

There is an important kind of wisdom in Levinson's work, a wisdom that illumines and teaches us to take seriously the interplay of being and time. He teaches us to see our own lives and those of others as evolutionary processes—as slowly unfolding tapestries requiring our best efforts at discernment, judgment, and evaluation. He warns us against choosing to submit our lives to changes and plunges too abruptly. He warns us against any cavalier uprooting and jostling around of our lives. He knows that deep-going changes in our lives, even as the result of conversion experiences, take months and years of integrative and reintegrative work. He cautions us not to be in too big a hurry but to fully engage the challenges and opportunities of each of our lives' seasons. And he suggests, by his analyses and theories, that we ought to take ourselves, our life decisions and commitments, very, very seriously. In a way that religious persons sometimes find offensive, Levinson calls for a brand of cool realism regarding our desires and requirements as to what will make our life structures livable and truly satisfactory.

Moreover, Levinson's approach counsels realism in another way as well. He knows that all life structures are going to be flawed and unsatisfactory in some important ways. There is no perfect job, no perfect marriage, no perfect balancing of personal and public life. There is no easy dealing with the tension of love of self and love of neighbor. His work counsels us to think in terms of modest and incremental changes in our lives rather than trying to fix things in some sudden, dramatic, and supposedly final change. Like the wisdom literature, Levinson knows that, in some sense, the more things change, the more they stay the same.

I do not find in Levinson any suggestion, as we find in the writings of Carl Jung, that persons in transition rely on the guiding power of the psyche or the psyche's own deep movements of spirit and symbol. Certainly there is no talk of reliance upon the guidance of the Holy Spirit. Instead, Levinson calls for a combination of rational reflection, consideration for the impact of our choices on others, and for thoughtful experimentation with our lives, guided by our own real desires and feelings. In Levinson's view, a person is finally accountable neither to society nor to God for the quality or direction of his or her pursuit of a dream. We are accountable finally to ourselves, he implies, for the satisfactoriness of our life structures and life cycle. He offers us an invitation to a kind of realism and candor, and he calls on us not to fool ourselves with the shoulds and oughts of others. His ethical approach is a brand of utilitarianism—a utilitarian calculus focused on our own individual interests and values. Choices and decisions are satisfactory if, in the long run (and Levinson anticipates at least four long seasons), they contribute to the prospects of our own satisfaction with the course and quality of our lives.

3. CAROL GILLIGAN: TWO PATHS TO RESPONSIBLE SELFHOOD

Carol Gilligan is younger and less well known than Erik Erikson or Daniel Levinson, but she is emerging very rapidly as a voice who must be taken seriously. She has written a book called *In a Different Voice: Psychological Theory and Women's Development*.[10] In order to grasp what Gilligan can offer us in our assessment of developmental psychological images of human wholeness, we have to reflect a bit on some of the work of her Harvard colleague and friend, Lawrence Kohlberg. For twenty years Kohlberg has studied and written about human development in the capacity to make moral judgments. His research has proceeded by giving people of all ages and several different cultures moral dilemmas, to which he asks them to respond. On the basis of their oral responses to stories that pose classical moral problems, Kohlberg and his associates have identified a sequence of structural stages that characterize the *ways* people perceive and reason about moral issues. He has done impressive empirical research in the effort to validate his claims that this sequence of stages is invariant and is found in all cultures in which he or his associates have made investigations.

Kohlberg has intentionally and responsibly related his empirical findings to Western traditions of moral philosophy and ethics. He has boldly claimed that each empirical stage represents a philosophical advance over the previous ones and that each later stage is, in some important ways, "better"—in the sense of being more comprehensively and consistently just than the preceding ones. Thus he has claimed that the sequence of stages he has described is not only descriptive but also normative.[11]

Over the years of Kohlberg's research, he and his associates, both male and female, gradually began to note a curious pattern in the stage assignments given to women's responses to the moral dilemmas. A much larger number of women than men were assigned to Kohlberg's Stage 3, the Interpersonal Concordance or Mutual Interpersonal Relations stage. This is a stage in which a person's moral judgments—and implicitly, one's sense of self—are derived from the requirements of social roles and the expectations of valued others. Relative to males in the sample, there were very few females assigned to Kohlberg's Stage 4, the Social System and Conscience stage. Stage 4 requires taking the perspective of the larger society, seeing it as a network of sometimes conflicting rules and roles. Stage 4 moral reasoning requires a kind of self-reflectiveness that enables one to balance and sort out the requirements of rules, roles, and relational requirements. The relatively small number of females in the Kohlberg sample who were assigned beyond Stage 3 tended to be assigned to Stage 5, the Social Contract Orientation Stage, rather than to Stage 4.

Gilligan and some of the other women related to Kohlberg's Center for Moral Development at Harvard University began to look more closely at the types of responses females typically gave to the Kohlberg dilemmas.[12] They began to note some significant differences between the responses of males and females. The "Heinz Dilemma" is a well-known hypothetical story Kohlberg has used widely in his research. In the story Heinz, a European, has a wife who is dying from a form of cancer. A druggist in Heinz's community has conducted research and developed a drug that is effective in curing the kind of cancer Mrs. Heinz has. Heinz tries to purchase the drug. Although the radium from which he makes the drug costs the druggist only $200, he asks $2,000 for the drug. Heinz exerts every effort but can only come up with $1,000. The druggist refuses to let him have it for that. Heinz grows desperate. The dilemma presentation concludes with the question "Should Heinz steal the drug?"

In response to this question, most boys and men tended to answer yes or no, and then go on, under questioning and probing, to give the justification for their particular answer. When girls and women were given the dilemma, however, frequently they countered with a number of questions themselves: "What is the relationship between Heinz and his wife?" "How are Heinz and his wife related to the larger community?" "Who in the larger community can they depend upon as their friends?" And "Who could influence the druggist to change his judgment?" "Who might help them raise the money?" And so on. Faced with these kinds of questions, researchers had been trained to say that the details of the story could not be questioned or changed: "Just take the dilemma and give your best judgment about what Heinz should do." In a sense, the instructions implied that women and others who raised these kinds of questions were simply evading the issue—refusing to "bite the bullet." Those who responded in these ways tended to be assigned to the Interpersonal Concordance stage.

Eventually Gilligan and others began to question why so many women seemed to be "stuck" in Stage 3, if indeed they were. They began to look more closely at the logic that women used as they responded to the set dilemmas. As they reconsidered the logic of women's responses, Gilligan and others began to discern and to suspect that perhaps women were perceiving and interpreting those moral situations in fundamentally different ways than most men. In Gilligan's view, the logic typical of women was no less developed, no less sophisticated, than that of men, but it was very, very different.

Intrigued by these tentative insights, Gilligan set out to pursue independent research on women. She chose to interview women with the standard Kohlberg dilemmas but also to interview them regarding real-life decisions they actually faced. As she attended to the data from three studies of this sort, gradually she began to be able to discern the contours of a different kind of moral interpretation and reasoning. Women, she began to see, seem to approach situations of moral choice with a tendency to see the actors and the affected parties in the situation as woven together in a web of relationships that has a history and an anticipated future—a web of relationships in time that can be expected to last. This web of relationships, which lasts and changes over time, entails responsibility for those in it to and for each other, as well as for the network of relationships taken as a whole. Decisions about moral actions, therefore, have to be made in terms of their impact on the total web of relations, in the present and in the future.

This relational logic that Gilligan found contrasted with the picture that Kohlberg had offered of the course of moral development based upon his initial research with some eighty boys and men. The males, as they developed, tended to emphasize the image and self-expectation of a growingly autonomous moral actor who approaches moral decision situations with the questions "What rules apply here?" "What rights are at stake here?" "What are my duties, or what are the duties of the other persons involved?" "What are my (or their) obligations?" and "What principle governs this kind of situation?" The basic image here is one of detachment from distorting values and relations and of trying to overcome the biases of personal involvement. In this logic, the way toward moral maturity leads in the direction of a kind of disinterestedness, an overcoming or offsetting of the biases of one's own interests and values. Moral maturity, as Kohlberg describes it, means advancement in the ability to take the perspectives of others, so as to be able more justly to balance their claims over against one's own claims. It means using principles that are essentially timeless and universal and trusting that such principles will yield just outcomes in any situation, if applied without the distortions of particular interests or affections. Moral maturity involves, thus, a kind of distancing of particular situations from factors of time and concreteness, as well as the effort to approach issues of moral disagreement with the aid of timeless and universal principles.

Let's look briefly at excerpts from two interviews reported by Gilligan that illustrate the two logics I have been describing. Both of these are with bright, articulate sixth graders: a boy, Jake, and a girl, Amy. Both were given the Heinz dilemma. Jake interpreted the dilemma as Kohlberg did—as a problem arising from the conflict of the values of human life versus property. From the outset he is clear that Heinz should steal the drug. In his justification he affirms the logical priority of life over property, and the issue is settled. Gilligan quotes Jake:

For one thing, a human life is worth more than money, and if the druggist only makes $1,000, he is still going to live, but if Heinz doesn't steal the drug, his wife is going to die. *(Why is life worth more than money?)* Because the druggist can get a thousand dollars later from rich people with cancer, but Heinz can't get his wife again. *(Why not?)* Because people are all different and so you couldn't get Heinz's wife again.[13]

Gilligan comments on Jake's response: "Fascinated by the power of logic, this eleven-year-old boy locates truth in math, which, he says, is 'the only thing that is totally logical.'" Jake said in the interview that he considered the moral dilemma to be "sort of like a math problem with humans." Gilligan again: "(Jake) sets it up as an equation and proceeds to work out the solution. Since his solution is rationally derived, he assumes that anyone following reason would arrive at the same conclusion . . ."[14]

Amy's response to the dilemma has a very different sound. She seems less sure of herself and is unable to come to a clear resolution of the dilemma as presented. Gilligan quotes from Amy's transcript when she is asked if Heinz should steal:

Well, I don't think so. I think there might be other ways besides stealing it, like if he could borrow the money or make a loan or something, but he really shouldn't steal the drug—but his wife shouldn't die either.[15]

Gilligan interjects an observation: "Asked why he should not steal the drug, she considers neither property nor law but rather the effect that theft could have on the relationship between Heinz and his wife:"

If he stole the drug, he might save his wife then, but if he did he might have to go to jail, and then his wife might get sicker again, and he couldn't get more of the drug, and it might not be good. So they should really just talk it out and find some other way to make the money.[16]

Gilligan's extended comment on Amy's responses needs to be quoted at length:

Seeing in the dilemma not a math problem with humans but a narrative of relationships that extends over time, Amy envisions the wife's continuing need for her husband and the husband's continuing concern for his wife and seeks to respond to the druggist's need in a way that would sustain rather than sever connection. Just as she ties the wife's survival to the preservation of relationships, so she considers the value of the wife's life in a context of relationships, saying that it would be wrong to let her die because, "if she died, it hurts a lot people and it hurts her." Since Amy's moral judgment is grounded in the belief that, "if somebody has something that would keep somebody alive, then it's not right not to give it to them," she considers the problem in the dilemma to arise not from the druggist's assertion of rights but from his failure of response.[17]

Gilligan has called the approach that she find more typical of women "the ethics of responsibility." We might characterize the approach that Kohlberg represents as "the ethics of duty or obligation." If you are a student of the history of theological and philosophical ethics, you will recognize that these two broad alternatives are not new. You will see analogues between Gilligan's position, with its ethics of responsibility, and the work of theologian H. Richard Niebuhr, whose book *The Responsible Self*,[18] develops very powerfully the notion of the self in time and relationships, construing moral situations in terms of shared interpretations and anticipating the responding actions of persons in the future. You will also think, perhaps, of the "ethics of character" as developed by theologians James Gustafson, James William McClendon, Stanley Hauerwas, and Craig Dykstra, and by philosophers Iris Murdoch and Alasdair MacIntyre. Gilligan has read Niebuhr; I suspect, however, that theologically the work of Martin Buber has been more decisive for her.

Theological analogues with Kohlberg's work would point to traditions of the ethics of God's command, such as those of Emil Brunner and the young Karl Barth. Philosophically, the ethics of duty and obligation achieved clearest expression in the work of Immanuel Kant. Contemporary representatives of deontological approaches of this sort would include John Rawls' Ideal Contractual theory of Justice, and the Ideal Observer theory of Roderick Firth.

I give these analogues to Gilligan and Kohlberg's work, not to drop names, but to point out that in identifying these two dominant modes of approaching moral decision making, I am not sug-gesting—nor is Gilligan—that we must choose between these al-ternatives, that one is necessarily better than the other, or that one should supplant the other. I do support Gilligan's affirmation, however, that we should no longer make the mistake of consider-ing the approach that she finds to be more typical of women to be less developed or more muddled than the other.

Now we come to an intriguing set of questions: Why is it that the approach we have called the "ethics of responsibility" seems more typically to characterize women in our society than men? And why is it that Kohlberg and others found males developing a sequence of moral stages that involved separations, autonomy, and the ethics of rights, duties, and obligations? Gilligan has asked these questions, and she has found the suggestive beginnings of some answers in recent psychoanalytic writings. These answers have to do with early childhood relations between mothers and their sons, and between mothers and their daughters. Gilligan draws here on the work of Nancy Chodorow[19] and Robert Stol-ler[20] who, separately, have done some helpful work on the forma-tion of gender identity.

Female identity formation, they tell us, occurs in the context of girls' ongoing relationships with their mothers. Mothers tend to experience their daughters as more like them and as more continu-ous with themselves than their sons. This means that girls are encouraged to experience themselves as being like their mothers. Consequently, they have a greater likelihood to find attachment and identification with the mother a natural way to grow. Boys, on the other hand, tend to be experienced by their mothers as being more nearly opposite or different from themselves. In the socialization of sons, these researchers suggest, mothers treat them differently from the start. They are given strong cues, by the mothers and others, that start them on a path toward gender iden-tity that requires separation and a certain kind of dis-identification with their mothers. They have to curtail, in this separation, some of the modes of their primary love for and empathetic ties with their mothers. Chodorow and Stoller suggest that this dis-identification and separation are more traumatic and difficult for boys than we often have realized. Male development, therefore, entails from the beginning a more emphatic differentiation and separation from the maternal person and a more defensive firming of experienced ego boundaries than does the development of the female child.

Nancy Chodorow draws some conclusions from the foregoing considerations. She says it is not the case that girls and women develop weaker ego boundaries than boys, due to these different experiences of coming to gender identity. But it does seem that girls emerge with empathy and capacities for closeness to others more centrally built into their ways of being selves. These considerations seem to give to the females, when compared to their male counterparts, a stronger (and less disrupted) basis for experiencing another's needs and feelings and for being in emotional solidarity with others. Moreover, empathetic identification with other persons should consequently be less threatening to the egos of girls than it often seems to be for boys. For the latter, given their history of painful and dangerous separation from the maternal matrix, empathy and intimacy can be experienced as a kind of threat of regression to a unity with their mothers, which feels dangerously like the threat of the loss of self.

I want to raise a critical issue with Gilligan and her psychoanalytic informants in just a moment. Before that, however, let's sum up the implications of this discussion of patterns of female and male gender identity formation: Throughout childhood, adolescence, and into young adulthood, this analysis suggests, girls and women have a greater likelihood than boys of experiencing continuity regarding relationships of intimacy in their lives. Boys having had to develop harder boundaries on their egos in order to become separate selves, have had to learn the dynamics (and the defenses) that go with differentiation and separation. Females are likely, therefore, to find experiences of connectedness and solidarity more "natural" for them and to find separations and conflict more problematic. Boys, on the other hand, tend to find competition less threatening and more enjoyable, while connectedness and intimacy can give them problems. (Gilligan cites some fascinating research by Janet Lever on children's play. Lever found that while boys seemed to enjoy the disputes over rules in their games as much as the games themselves, girls more frequently stopped the games rather than wrangle over the rules. Gilligan concludes from this that the connections of friendship, which might be threatened by quarreling, are more important to the girls than competition or the games.)[21]

Now the critical question to Carol Gilligan: So far as I can tell, Gilligan has not given attention to the implications for a boy's development of a readiness for intimacy and care resulting from the effects of *paternal* care and example. Nor does she deal with paternal influences as a factor in a girl's ability to differentiate and stand alone. Both these considerations seem to be of fundamental importance. Gilligan herself is careful in her writing and speaking to make it clear that she is not making ironclad generalizations about *all* women or *all* men. She knows that there are many exceptions and that positions are taken by men and women all along a continuum in these matters. Further research that explicitly investigates sexual differences in moral development, including finding a way to include consideration of the salience of contributions by parents of *both* sexes, is badly needed. Such research may tend to qualify the suggestion of any necessarily sharp distinction between men and women's moral development.

Gilligan's contribution to our understanding of human wholeness and completion focuses especially on images of *moral* maturity. The implications of her work are that the morally mature woman or man is one who has moved through either the route of developing an ethics of responsibility or through the route of the ethics of rights and duties, to the point where the strengths of each of these positions approach each other and can be integrated. Her comments about the ideal trajectories of moral development for Jake and Amy help bring this into focus:

If the trajectory of development were drawn through either of these children's responses, it would trace a correspondingly different path. For

Jake, development would entail coming to see the other as equal to the self and the discovery that equality provides a way of making connections safe. For Amy, development would follow the inclusion of herself in an expanding network of connection and the discovery that separation can be protective and need not entail isolation. In view of these different paths of development and particularly of the different ways in which the experiences of separation and connection are aligned with the voice of the self, the representation of the boy's development as the single line of adolescent growth for both sexes creates a continual problem when it comes to interpreting the development of the girl.[22]

For women, the trajectory of moral development means learning to balance the rights of persons, *including their own rights,* over against the claims of the welfare of groups of persons for whom they feel responsible. It means developing a more detached capacity for employing rules and principles to determine just outcomes, when no action can be taken that will not harm someone. (This is part of the tragedy of moral decision making; we sometimes have to make moral decisions when no outcome can avoid harming someone.) For men, the trajectory toward moral wholeness means learning to think and feel more holistically, to overcome excessive detachment, and to learn to see persons in relationships and in the context of shared histories and mutual responsibilities. It means, for men, strengthening the ability to take responsibility and effective care of ongoing communities and webs of relationships.

Gilligan teaches us that moral maturity, for women and for men, means balancing responsibility and care with a keen sense of rights and justice, along with learning to deal with the inevitable tensions and ambiguities that this will involve. This may be an important dimension of the integration, in mature adulthood, of the masculine and the feminine modalities in our lives.

NOTES

1. Erik H. Erikson, *Childhood and Society,* (First Edition). New York: W. W. Norton, 1950. (Second Edition, 1963).
2. For perspectives on Erikson's authorship and life, see Erik Erikson, *Life History*

and the Historical Moment (New York: Norton, 1975), chap. 1; see also Robert Coles, Erik H. Erikson, The Growth of His Work (Boston: Little Brown, 1970).

3. See Erik Erikson, Identity and the Life-Cycle: A Reissue (New York: Norton, 1980), pp. 51–107.

4. The classic statement of Erikson's Eight Ages is to be found in Erik Erikson, Childhood and Society, 2nd ed. (New York: Norton, 1963), chap. 7.

5. Don S. Browning, Generative Man: Psychoanalytic Perspectives (Philadelphia: Westminster Press, 1972).

6. Ibid.

7. Daniel J. Levinson et al., The Seasons of a Man's Life (New York: Knopf, 1978), pp. 6–7.

8. Ibid.

9. Bernice Neugarten, "Adult Personality: Toward a Psychology of the Life Cycle" in William C. Sze, Ed., Human Life Cycle. New York: Jason Aronson Inc., 1975, p. 389.

10. Carol Gilligan, In a Different Voice: Psychological Theory and Women's Development (Cambridge: Harvard University Press, 1982).

11. See Lawrence Kohlberg, The Philosophy of Moral Development (San Francisco: Harper & Row, 1981).

12. For accounts of the rise and evaluation of critiques of Kohlberg's theory and research on the basis of its inclusiveness, see the following: James R. Rest, Development in Judging Moral Issues (Minneapolis: University of Minnesota Press, 1979) pp. 120–24; Ann Colby, "Listening to a Different Voice: A Book Review" (prepublication draft); John C. Gibbs, Kevin Arnold, and Jennifer E. Burkhart, "Sex-Differences in the Expression of Moral Judgment." (prepublication draft); Mary Brabeck, "Moral Judgment: Theory and Research in Differences Between Males and Females," Developmental Review Vol. III, Number 3, 1983, pp. 274–291.

13. Gilligan, In a Different Voice, p. 26.

14. Ibid., pp. 26–27.

16. Ibid., p. 28.

17. Ibid.

18. H. Richard Niebuhr, The Responsible Self (New York: Harper & Row, 1963).

19. See Nancy Chodorow, "Family Structures and Feminine Personality," in M. Z. Rosaldo and L. Lampher, eds., Women, Culture and Society (Stanford: Stanford University Press, 1974); and Nancy Chodorow, The Reproduction of Mothering (Berkeley: University of California Press, 1978).

20. See Robert J. Stoller, "A Contribution to the Study of Gender Identity," International Journal of Psycho-Analysis 45 (1964): 220–226.

21. Janet Lever, "Sex Differences in the Games Children Play," Social Problems 23 (1976): 478–487; and "Sex Differences in the Complexity of Children's Play and Games," American Sociological Review 43 (1978): 471–483.

22. Gilligan, In A Different Voice, p. 39.

III. Faith Development Theory and the Human Vocation

1. TAKING STOCK

Let's begin by bringing the discussion of the previous chapter into summary focus. With Erik Erikson, we examined the virtues and strengths that coalesce in mid-life in the qualities of generative personhood. His work lifts up the critical importance of finding ways, by mid-life at least, of employing one's gifts and abilities in long-term commitments to *care* for persons, for institutions, and for society, so that in one's own life cycle one contributes to the strengthening of the ongoing cycle of the generations.

Daniel Levinson's perspective enriches our understanding of life as process. In contrast to societal tendencies to overprize youth and young adulthood, he asserts the dignity, the creativity, and the richness that each of the four major seasons of our lives makes possible. Avoiding giving prescriptive norms for good woman-hood/manhood, Levinson, instead, provides a framework that can help us keep abreast of "what time it is in our lives" and understand some of the dynamics of transitional experiences. His position can help by providing one kind of orientation we need as we face decisions or choices and as we work at the maintenance and renewal of long-term commitments.

Carol Gilligan offers us insight into some specific dimensions of our growth as moral selves that may be different for women and men. More broadly, her writings caution us against the uncritical acceptance of *any* of these developmental "myths of becoming" as descriptive or normative for all persons. Gilligan helps us to see in fresh ways that human wholeness or completion requires a balance between responsibility and care for others (and their relatedness to each other), on the one hand, and regard and care for the self, on the other. For this balancing in our lives—not just in our minds—we need the virtues that come with connectedness, intimacy, love, and care. But we also need the virtue of fairness, a sense of justice, and a principled commitment to duty.

In our examination of developmental "myths of becoming" so far, we have restricted ourselves to research and theories that do not explicitly address questions of faith. Erikson, of course, acknowledges the importance of a religious or philosophical world view for expressing and grounding the conviction that life has meaning. But he does not consistently or in any comprehensive way focus on the role of faith—or the development of faith—in our life cycles. Levinson, surprisingly, has little to say about values or beliefs. Most of the persons written up in his studies and those of his team did not volunteer information about their faith. The interview protocols they followed did not seem to probe this area. Gilligan's work, like that of Kohlberg, tends to deal with moral development primarily in terms of moral perception and judgment. Although she has enlarged the research aperture to include images of the self, most of the characterizations of self she reports have to do with one's roles, the enumeration of distinguishing personal qualities, and one's aspirations and self-esteem. She and her colleagues have given no explicit attention to the meanings and images by which their respondents shape their responses and initiatives in life.

Turn with me now to consider the research and theory on faith development for which I and my associates have been primarily responsible. While I have written about this work extensively in other publications,[1] it is necessary to give a brief account of it here. This account will be different from previous ones in that our concern will be to clarify what faith development theory has to offer in our assessment of the normative visions of human wholeness offered by adult developmental theories.

2. FAITH, A FOCUS FOR RESEARCH

For more than ten years, I and a group of associates have been engaged in conducting and interpreting research that invites people of a variety of ages, of both sexes, and of many religious and secular orientations to inquire with us into the operations and themes of faith in their lives. We began this research with the premise that faith is a human universal. By this we mean that wherever we find human beings, our species is marked by several uniform features and dimensions of struggle and awareness. We are marked by the universal awareness of death—an awareness that we futilely endeavor to keep at an impersonal distance as much and as long as we can. We are marked with the burden of having to make life-defining choices under conditions of uncertainty and risk. Not only is this a matter of insufficient experience or inadequate information, but we also live, choose, react, and respond under the sentence of *contingency* and under some degree of thralldom to the unknown and the unknowable. Moreover, we live with a disconcerting duality., We have imaginations, intuitions, and moments of awakening that disturb us into awareness of dimensions of circumambient reality that we can only name, on our own, as "mystery." And yet our feet mire in the clay of everyday toil—getting and giving, spending and being spent—in the struggle for survival and meaning. In the midst of contingency, suckled on uncertainty, we spend our blessed and threatened years becoming selves through relations of trust and loyalty with others like us—persons and communities. We attach to each other in love; we struggle with each other in fidelity and infidelity. We share our visions of ultimate destiny and calling, our projections in hope, our moments of revelation in awe, and our fear in numbness or protest. We are language-related, symbol-borne and story-sustained creatures. We do not live long or well without meaning.

That is to say, we are creatures who live by faith. We live by forming and being formed in images and dispositions toward the ultimate conditions of our existence. And for at least 300 millennia these images and dispositions have been the province of religion.

Faith has been religious faith, from the first red ocher and flower-decked cave burials to Chartres Cathedral. Issues of faith have been named and addressed through the mediation of religion—the collective expressions through rite, myth, symbol, ethical teachings, and music, of human apprehensions of and by the holy.

The modern period, however, has been marked by the rise of scientism and the breakdown, for many, of their communal groundings in shared narratives of meaning. Secularization, the rise of pluralism, and the vertigo of relativity have all cracked and fissured the mosaics of meaning by which whole cultures have been formed and sustained. We have come to recognize that the activity of being and becoming in faith may take forms and may struggle for integrity in directions other than through cultic or institutional religion. There are secular forms and objects of faith. There are secular communities of faith. There are stances toward the limiting conditions of human life that are idiosyncratic, if not to say solipsistic. A kind of modern parallel to the situation after the destruction of the biblical Tower of Babel[2] prevails. Each person or small subculture struggles to form and maintain a shelter of shared values and life-style that will provide protection against the quicksand of meaninglessness and the winds and terrors of cosmic aloneness. And for many, narcotization is the solution—the forgetting, the ignoring, or the escape through consumption or distraction of the burdens of our finite vulnerability. Or in the form most favored by a culture that believes its own distorted myths of individualism, there is the effort, through the acquisition of stuff, power, or "securities," or through achievements or relationships, to negate our vulnerability and to outfox fate.

Over the past ten years, in a variety of settings, we have conducted in-depth, semiclinical interviews, with approximately 500 persons.[3] Among other interests, we have sought to test whether certain developmental patterns that seem to hold in the domains of cognitive, psychosocial, and moral growth have developmental parallels in this area of faith. Our underlying questions have been these: How do persons awaken to and begin to form (and be formed) in the life stances of trust and loyalty, of belief and commitment that carry them into the force fields of their lives? Are there predictable stages or revolutions in the life of meaning-making? Must we, in order to become fully adult and to be fully human, have a deep-going and abiding trust in and loyalty to some cause or causes, greater in value and importance than ourselves?

3. STAGES OF FAITH AND HUMAN BECOMING

In the analysis of these faith development interviews, which may last up to three hours with adults, we have found suggestive grounds for proposing a sequence of stagelike ways of being in faith in order to describe a general pattern of development in faith. These stages, which try to describe uniform and predictable *ways* of being in faith, are not primarily matters of the *contents* of faith. We are not suggesting that a person goes through a succession of world views and value systems, if we mean by those terms substantive beliefs, themes, images, and stories of faith. Rather, we are trying to identify and communicate differences in the *styles,* the *operations of knowing and valuing,* that constitute the action, the way of being that is faith. Our stages describe in formal terms the structural features of faith as a way of construing, interpreting, and responding to the factors of contingency, finitude, and ultimacy in our lives.

Let's look at the seven stages of faith that we have identified.[4]

Primal Faith. We start as infants, you and I. Someone picks us up, wipes off our afterbirth, and provides a nipple with breast or bottle, and we are launched as human beings. Prior to the event of birth itself, we have enjoyed one of the most remarkable of symbiotic relationships. Somatically, we likely have already derived from our life in the womb some sense of whether the world that welcomes us has meaning and purpose, and whether it intended and rejoices in our presence, or whether we come as intruders. Birth itself is a trauma. Students of the birth process tell us that even in the twenty-minute passage through the birth canal in a normal birth, we nearly smother. There is a threat of negation in our emergence into life. We are bruised and squeezed into life; we gasp our way into community.

During the first year, the mutual tasks of the baby and those providing care involve bonding and attachment, as well as the generation of a trusting give-and-take. Such a wondrous process! The baby's early efforts at relating and making the self at home have the effect, when things go well, of recruiting tenderness and mobilizing energetic care. In the mutuality of need and the need to be needed, the baby forms a rudimentary but deep sense of the rhythms of intimacy and of the texture of his or her environment. Without a reflexive sense of selfhood yet, it nonetheless—in the undifferentiated state that Ulric Neisser calls the "ecological self" —begins to wrap the coils of centration around primal images of the felt goodness and badness of *self-world*.[5] Basic trust versus a sense of basic mistrust, Erik Erikson described it. The struggle is for some balance of trust in the worth and irreplaceability of the self and in the "rely-ability" of the environment made up of those in whose eyes and under whose care the mirrored self has begun to gather. Paul Tillich called our inevitable sense of vulnerability to dropping out of being "ontological anxiety"—the anxiety that comes with being and with the threat of nonbeing.[6] Primal faith arises in the roots of confidence that find soil in the ecology of relations, care, and shared meanings that welcome a child and offset our profound primal vulnerability.

The first symbols of faith are likely to take primitive form in the baby's hard-won memories of maternal and paternal presence. As dependable realities who go away but can be trusted to return, our primary care givers constitute our first experiences of superordinate power and wisdom, as well as our dependence. These primal others, in their mixtures of rigidity and grace, of arbitrary harshness and nurturing love, are doubtless present in the images of God that take more or less conscious form by our fourth or fifth years.[7]

Intuitive-Projective Faith. About age two a revolution begins to happen for the child. Language emerges to mediate relations to the world and others in new ways. Important preparation for this emergence has gone on in the interchanges between the child and those providing primary care, where—as videotapes of mother-child interactions show—each is teaching the other to talk. The mothers' imitations of the facial expressions and vocal experiments of their babies seem to provide a crucial mirror—both visually and vocally. And as the children match sounds and objects, they gain new leverage in communication and in the interpretation of the world. Language makes possible a qualitatively new reflectiveness on the environment and a qualitatively new reflexiveness with regard to the self.

The child, now able to walk freely and question everything, daily encounters novelties and newness. Whether we remember the vividness of our daily (and nightly) delights and terrors at three, four, and five or whether we have access to it only by observing others now in childhood, we know that the active, inquiring mind of the child will never again be so fresh and free of preformed constructions. Perception, feelings, and imaginative fantasy make up children's principal ways of knowing—and transforming—their experiences. The ordering tendencies of logical operations will come later. For now, stimulated by experience and by stories, symbols, and examples, children form deep and long-lasting images that hold together their worlds of meaning and wonder.

While the following statement would never be said this way by a child, this effort to synthesize some of the feelings and imagery of Intuitive-Projective faith is suggestive:[8]

I feel like I am the center of the world. Everything important to me is there because of me, to be for me. When we travel at night, the moon follows just our car. Flowers are there to smell with, and stars are there to fly to.

Sometimes I have scary dreams at night. They are right there in my room. If you were in the room with me, you could see them too. Sometimes during the daytime I think about things like are in my dreams. Sometimes they make me scared.

I wonder sometimes where heaven is and what being dead means. If it is like a monster taking people away, or if it hurts, or if mommy and daddy will be with me. What happened to our pet bird the neighbor's cat got?

My friend told me that the devil will come up out of a hole in the ground and get me if I'm not careful, so now I won't play in the backyard by myself.

I think about God a lot. I think God must be like the air—everywhere. Can God see me? Will God help keep our house from fire? Is granddad with God? Where's that?

Here we see the Intuitive-Projective child's awakening to the mystery of death. We see the awakening to a world of reality beyond, around, and penetrating the everyday. We see lively imagination grasping the world, endeavoring to give it unity and sense. The preschool child who has access to the symbols, stories, and shared liturgical life of a religious tradition awakens to an expanded horizon of meanings. Though such symbols, in their archetypal power, can be misused (for example, the devil imagery in the previous quote), they also enrich the child's stores of meaning and can provide powerful identifications and aspirations, as well as sources of guidance and reassurance.

Mythic-Literal Faith. At about the time a child starts to school (six or seven, give or take a year), we see the beginnings of a new stage. Part of the groundwork for this revolution in knowing and valuing relates to the development of what Piaget called "concrete operational thinking." Stable categories of space, time, and causality make the child's constructions of experience much less dependent on feeling and fantasy. Now able to reverse processes of thought and to coordinate more than one feature of a situation at a time, the world becomes more linear, orderly, and predictable. Children in this stage routinely take the perspectives of others on matters of mutual interest, and they recognize others' perspectives as different from their own. This means that they can tell stories with new accuracy and richness. It also means that in their thinking about right and wrong, good and evil, they can develop a strong sense of fairness based on reciprocity (this means elevating the associations of reward for doing good and punishment for doing bad to the level of cosmic principle).

Faith becomes a matter of reliance on the stories, rules, and implicit values of the family's community of meanings. Where the family (or its substitute) is related to a larger community of shared traditions and meanings, faith involves valuing the stories, practices, and beliefs of that tradition. *Narrative* or story is the important idea here. With the abilities to take the perspectives of others and with a much-improved grasp of causal relations and consequences, narrative seems to be the favored and most powerful way of gathering and expressing personal and shared meanings. Knowing the stories of "our people" becomes an important index of identification and of evaluation of self and others and their groups. The ability to create classes based on distinguishing characteristics of objects or groups makes these kinds of identifications (and exclusions) important matters in this stage.

The following composite passage suggests some flavor of how the Mythic-Literal child typically describes self and faith.

You asked me who I am: I'll tell you. I am Robert Kelleher, the son of Tom and Diane, and the brother of Kristen and Kevin. Do you want me to tell you about all my grandparents and cousins too? No? Well . . . , uh, I'm a member of Mrs. Cates's fourth-grade class at Hawthorne School . . . uh, and I am third-best soccer player in my grade, after Donald Pruitt and Teddy Jackson. Oh yes, uh, I go to Christ the King parish. My scout troop meets there—it's troop 27, Cub Scouts, that is. Well, that's about it.

Yes, I believe in God. What is God like? Hmm . . . Well, I guess God is like Jesus, sort of . . . . We believe that God is, like, in three parts, Father, Son, and, um . . . , Spirit—*Holy* Spirit. But I picture God mostly as Jesus. But sometimes I sort of think of God as an old man, and sort of like a judge or ruler . . . . Yes, God made us and loves us and wants us to love each other. I think the worst thing God doesn't like is all the nuclear bombs. I would like to tell all the presidents of the world, "Don't use those bombs. Let us grow up. Let the earth, the grass, and all the animals continue to live."

The most important thing is not to tell lies and to stick up for your friends if they need help. Like when my best friend Roger got into trouble last week. The teacher who monitors the hall thought that . . . well, you see, this locker got broken into and some stuff was stolen from it, and, uh, the hall teacher thought she saw Roger taking some stuff from the broken locker, and he *did* have a Walkman just like the one that was stolen, so the principal called him in because they thought Roger did it. Roger didn't deserve that! Well, I went straight to the principal and told him it was not Roger, that he already had a Walkman that he got for his birthday, and besides that, Roger would never steal anything. The principal really listened to me, and he and the teacher apologized to Roger.

In these statements we hear something of the concreteness and literalness of this boy's appropriation of his community's beliefs. We also see that he does not construct either his sense of himself or of others in terms of personality or inner feelings and reflectiveness. Persons are defined by their affiliations and their actions. He speaks to us from in the midst of the flowing stream of his life, without stepping out onto the bank to reflect on its overall direction or meanings. He does not yet have a "story of his stories." His poignant statement about the threat of nuclear warfare is *powerfully typical* of our interviews with children in this stage.

We do, from time to time, encounter adults whose ways of structuring their faith have features very similar to Robert's. A substantial number of adolescents share his way of constructing their images of self, others, and ultimate environment. From this stage on, we are dealing with ways of being in faith that *can* typify adults as well as the age groups where they most typically have their rise.

Synthetic-Conventional Faith. We come now to a stage that typically begins to emerge in early adolescence. Before we discuss its particular features, it may be helpful to inject a few observations about the phenomenon of stage transition. It would be a mistake to think of the movement from one faith stage to another as analogous to climbing stairs or ascending a ladder, for two reasons: (1.) It unnecessarily locks us into a kind of "higher"-"lower" mentality in thinking about the stages, when the real issue has to do with a successive progression of more complex, differentiated, and comprehensive modes of knowing and valuing. (2.) The stair or ladder analogy, further, might lead us to think of transition as a matter of the self clambering from one level or rung to another, essentially unchanged. Faith stage transitions represent significant alterations in the structures of one's knowing and valuing and, therefore, in the basic orientation and responses of the self. In the process of transition we have the feeling, as one character in the film *Green Pastures* put it, that "everything nailed down is coming loose." Because of new operations and comprehensiveness in our knowing and valuing, both our previous knowledge and values and our very ways of verifying and justifying our perspectives and our actions undergo change and must be reworked. Our very life meanings are at stake in faith stage transitions. In relation to the transition we are just considering—from the Mythic-Literal to the Synthetic-Conventional stage—let me share an example. We have interviewed a number of what we have come to call "eleven-year-old athiests." These young people, almost on the cusp between concrete operational thinking and formal operational thinking (a Piagetian term we will examine more fully in a moment), begin to experience the breakdown of the moral principle of reciprocity that they frequently have used to compose their images of God. By observation and experience, they have found that either God is powerless, with regard to punishing evil people and rewarding the good, or God is, as one morally sensitive girl put it, "asleep." The God, therefore, who is constructed on the basis of moral reciprocity effectively dies and must be replaced. Such an experience involves, to a greater or lesser degree, coming to terms with feelings of anguish, struggle, and possibly guilt and grief. This is the stuff of which faith stage transitions are made.

Now to Synthetic-Conventional faith. The key to our understanding the structure and dynamics of this stage is an appreciation for a revolution that adolescence typically brings in cognitive development. In formal operational thinking the mind takes wings. No longer is it limited to the mental manipulation of concrete objects or representations and of observable processes. Now thinking begins to construct all sorts of ideal possibilities and hypothetical considerations. Faced with the challenge of developing the perfect mousetrap, the formal operational mind doesn't limit itself to modifying and perfecting the type of mousetraps it has seen, but it starts with the fundamental problem of disposing of a household pest and imagines a great variety of ways the problem might be solved. Imagination, one writer has said, is intelligence at play. Formal operational thinking makes possible the generation and use of abstract concepts and ideals. It makes it possible to think in terms of systems. And it enables us to construct the perspectives of others on ourselves—to see ourselves as others see us. Part of the confusion and difficulty of adolescence can be traced to the new self-consciousness I have summed up with the following couplet:

> I see you seeing me . . .
> I see the me I think you see. . . .

And its reciprocal:

> You see you according to me . . .
> You see the you you think I see. . . .

Putting these two together as elements of consciousness (which takes a period of several months, at least) results in what students of perspective taking have called "mutual interpersonal perspective taking." This emergence accounts for the "self-consciousness" of adolescence. It accounts for the rather sudden new depth of awareness and interest in the interiority (emotions, personality patterns, ideas, thoughts, and experiences) of persons—others and oneself. It makes for a newly "personal" young woman or man.

Synthetic, as we use the term here, does not mean *artificial.* Rather it means pulling together and drawing disparate elements into a unity, a synthesis. The drawing together in question is twofold. Due to the rich new possibilities of interpersonal perspective taking, the young person now has available a variety of reflections or mirrorings of the self. In every significant face-to-face relation, he or she has access to someone's construction of the self he/she is becoming. Like distorting mirrors in an amusement park fun house, the images of self that one discerns that others have constructed do not necessarily fit nicely together. Nor are they necessarily congruent with one's own felt images of self. Saint Augustine, writing about his own adolescent experience in this stage, said, "And I became a problem to myself." Synthesis, in the first instance then, means a drawing together, an integration into one, of that viable sense in selfhood that we have come to call "identity."

The other aspect of synthesis crucial to the forming of the Synthetic-Conventional stage has to do with the drawing together of one's stories, values, and beliefs into a supportive and orienting unity. In this stage a person struggles with composing a "story of my stories"—a sense of the meaning of life generally and of the meaning and purpose of her/his life in particular. Our research suggests that this involves a process of drawing together into an original unity a selection of the values, beliefs, and orienting convictions that are made available to the adolescent through her/his significant face-to-face relations. Although each person's worldview synthesis in this stage is in some degree unique, we describe it as "conventional" for two important reasons: (1.) It is a synthesis of belief and value elements that are derived from one's significant others. The elements themselves, then, are conventional, although they may be formed into a novel, individual configuration. (2.) It is a synthesis of belief and value that has, in this stage, a largely "tacit" (as opposed to "explicit") character. By this we mean that the beliefs, values, and stories that compose a person's faith outlook and support her/his emerging identity are not yet objectified for critical reflection by that person. The synthesis is supportive and sustaining; it is deeply felt and strongly held; but it has not yet become an object of (self) critical reflection and inquiry. In this stage one is *embedded* in her/his faith outlook, and one's identity is derived from membership in a circle of face-to-face relations.

Consider the following composite statement from a fifteen-year-old girl:

My life is so full of people! And it seems like all of them want something special from me. Start with my best friend: She wants me to spend at least an hour a day on the telephone with her. She would like it if we sat together in all our classes and ate lunch together everyday. Her parents are moving toward a divorce, she doesn't have a boyfriend, and all her other brothers and sisters have left home. But that's just the beginning. There's Sam. He's *my* boyfriend. He's a year older than I. *He* wants me to spend all my time between classes and at lunch with him. And then he wants to bring me home from school everyday and talk on the phone every night. We fight a lot—not about your usual thing—who's jealous of whom, etc.—but about beliefs and values. He tries, but he comes from a family where male chauvinism reigns supreme. He is the last child—and the first son—and he has always been spoiled terribly. Then he has this romantic nonsense about chivalry and male honor and superiority. We argue and debate and even shout at each other on the phone.

Then there's my parents. Since my older sister went off to college, we have been very close. I know that they have high expectations of me. Even though they don't say too much about it directly, they always ask questions like "how was your day? . . . how did your test go? . . . how are things with Sam? . . ." and so on. They don't mean it to be pressure, but it makes me feel that there are a lot of demands on me.

Then there are my teachers, my friends at church, my flute teacher, my grandparents, and my sister. All of them, in one way or another, want a piece of me, or symbolize some set of demands I make on myself. And yet, I wonder if any of them really know *me?*

I don't think any of them know, really, about my relation to God. I don't think of God as an old man, or even a person, anymore. Instead, I have this deep feeling that God is a kind of friend, a presence that loves me, cares for me, and *really* knows me. God knows me—my present me, and my future me—even better than I know myself. When I wake up early in the mornings—4:00 A.M. most mornings—to study, in the loneliness and tiredness there is God. When I feel on the outs with my parents, or Sam, or my friends, there is God. When I feel that I will *never* be good enough in math and chemistry to get into veterinarian school, there is God.

I don't speak of God as "He" anymore. In the Apostles' Creed I say "Creator" instead of "Father." But other than that, I think my church's teachings about God are true and good—especially my teacher Mr. Martin. He knows so much, and has so much enthusiasm, and makes it all so clear. I just wish my church lived up to all it knows!

It is important to recognize that many persons equilibrate in the Synthetic-Conventional stage. The world view and sense of self synthesized in this stage and the authorities who confirm one's values and beliefs are internalized, and the person moves on through the life cycle with a set of tacitly held, strongly felt, but largely unexamined beliefs and values. Our fifteen-year-old girl, quoted in the composite statement above, however, gives evidence already that she will likely make another transition in her faith and identity in her early adulthood—the transition to what we call the Individuative-Reflective stage of faith.

Individuative-Reflective Faith. In the previous stage it is very difficult to engage in pulling together unified images of identity and faith and at the same time to critically reflect on those images. This is what accounts for the tacit character of the faith of persons best described as Synthetic-Conventional.

The rise of Individuative-Reflective faith is occasioned by a variety of experiences that make it necessary for persons to objectify, examine, and make critical choices about the defining elements of their identity and faith. Two fundamental movements are at the heart of a transition to this stage: (1) There must be a shift in the sense of the grounding and orientation of the self. From a definition of self derived from one's relations and roles and the network of expectations that go with them, the self must now begin to be and act from a new quality of self-authorization. There must be the emergence of an "executive ego"—a differentiation of the self *behind* the personae (masks) one wears and the roles one bears, from the composite of roles and relations through which the self is expressed. (2) There must be an objectification and critical choosing of one's beliefs, values, and commitments, which come to be taken as a systemic unity. What were previously tacit and unexamined convictions and beliefs must now become matters of more explicit commitment and accountability.

The following composite statement from a young adult woman should give this description more concreteness. She might well be our fifteen-year-old girl from the last stage, only ten years later.

It is important to me to be able to know and state my beliefs and my values. I have had to face and struggle toward and answer to the question

"Who am I when I'm not defined by being my parents' daughter, the friend of my friends, by my job, or by any other of the roles I play?" There is an "I" that *has* these roles but is not identical with any of them. I guess it is this I that organizes the many roles I play and the relations I have. And I have had to struggle hard to get it established!

I went through a time when I realized that there are many different groups of people with many different life-styles and value systems. For a while I came to believe that these matters— life-styles and belief systems— were all matters of relativity. While I didn't like the idea, I was not sure that my reasons for being committed to my values and beliefs were any better than those of anyone else. Maybe, I thought, relativism *is* the only truth. But I found that I couldn't live that way.

So I have made choices—choices about my beliefs and values, about life-style, and about the groups I will be part of and those I won't. I feel like I have "gotten it together," as they say. And now I am working to bring my beliefs and my living together.

In the process of clarifying my beliefs, I have had to examine some of the doctrines and myths of my religious tradition. I have learned that literalism or disbelief are not the only alternatives for dealing with the biblical story of creation or with the miracles of Jesus. The important thing is the *meanings* that are being conveyed in these stories from another cultural time. These meanings are valuable and indispensable. But they are separable, in some sense, from the outmoded, mythical world views that contain them in the Bible.

So I'm trying to achieve integrity in my faith. It's not so easy. And a lot of people think that I'm crazy to hang in with religion. Others in my church think that I raise too many questions and rock the boat too much. But I've found a few people who share my questions—and some of my answers—and we make our way.

While this young woman has struggled toward the Individuative stage in her early and midtwenties, for many others this transition comes, if at all, only later. When individuals in their thirties or forties face this transition, it can be quite disturbing to the whole network of roles and relations they have formed. Sometimes people will work through only one of the two shifts we examined above. They will carry out the critical examination of beliefs and values and make choices in that regard but will not evolve the self-authorization of the "executive ego." Or they will evolve this sense of self-authorization but will not carry out a critical examination and regrounding of his system of values and beliefs. In either case, they will exhibit a kind of stabilized transitional position that is not fully describable by either the Synthetic or the Individuative position but is truly somewhere in between.

Conjunctive Faith. For some persons whom we have interviewed, at mid-life or beyond there seems to be a transition to a stage I have come to call "Conjunctive faith." This name can be traced to Nicholas of Cusa (1401–1464), whose greatest work, *De Docta Ignorantia,* developed the idea of God as the *coincidentia oppositorum*—"the coincidence of opposites"—the being wherein all opposites and contradictions meet and are reconciled. Carl Jung adapted this idea in many of his psychological writings on religion, altering the term to the *coniunctio oppositorum*—the "conjunction of opposites."[9] The stage of faith that emerges with mid-life or beyond involves the integration of elements in ourselves, in society, and in our experience of ultimate reality that have the character of being apparent contradictions, polarities, or at the least, paradoxical elements. Let me explain.

The hard-won integrity of the individuative stage is based upon a clear sense of reflective identity, a firm set of ego boundaries, and a confident regard for one's *conscious* sense of self as though it were virtually exhaustive of one's total selfhood. The experience of reaching mid-life (age thirty-five and beyond) for some people marks the onset of new dimensions of awareness that can precipitate the movement to a new stage, the stage of Conjunctive faith. In this transition the firm boundaries of the previous stage begin to become porous and permeable. The confident conscious ego must develop a humbling awareness of the power and influence of aspects of the unconscious on our reactions and behavior—the individual, the social, and the archetypal unconscious. Moreover, having lived with ourselves as adults for twenty years or more, we begin to have to come to terms with certain of our patterns of behavior that we may never be able fully to change.

By this time one has begun to have to deal with a new sense of the reality and the power of death. Peers and some who are younger have died. Perhaps parents, and certainly many of their generation, have died. One recognizes that he/she may have lived more than half of an expectable lifetime, and the unmistakable signs of irreversible aging are both felt and visible. One's children may now be teenagers or young adults. One probably feels the full weight of being a member of the "bridge" generation, the linking group between the elders, who are gradually passing off the scene, and the youth, who are just beginning to seek and find their entering points in being the generation of the future.

Hallmarks of the transition to Conjunctive faith include the following: (1.) An awareness of the need to face and hold together several unmistakable *polar tensions* in one's life: the polarities of being both *old* and *young* and of being both *masculine* and *feminine*. Further, it means integrating the polarity of being both *constructive* and *destructive* and the polarity of having both a *conscious* and a *shadow self*. (2.) Conjunctive faith brings a felt sense that truth is more multiform and complex than most of the clear, either-or categories of the Individuative stage can properly grasp. In its richness, ambiguity, and multidimensionality, truth must be approached from at least two or more angles of vision simultaneously. Like the discovery in physics that to explain the behavior of light requires two different and unreconcilable models—one based on the model of packets of energy and one based on the model of wave theory—Conjunctive faith comes to cherish paradox and the apparent contradictions of perspectives on truth as intrinsic to that truth. (3.) Conjunctive faith moves beyond the reductive strategy by which the Individuative stage interprets symbol, myth, and liturgy into conceptual meanings. Beyond demythologization and the critical translation of the mythic and symbolic to propositional statements, Conjunctive faith gives rise to a "second naïveté", a postcritical receptivity and readiness for participation in the reality brought to expression in symbol and myth. This means (4.) a genuine openness to the truths of traditions and communities other than one's own. This openness, however, is not to be equated with a relativistic agnosticism (literally, a "not knowing"). Rather, it is a disciplined openness to truths of those who are "other," based precisely on the experience of a deep and particular commitment to one's own tradition and the recognition that truth requires a dialectical interplay of such perspectives. Put another way, Conjunctive faith exhibits a combination of committed belief in and through the particularities of a tradition, while insisting upon the humility that knows that the grasp on ultimate truth that any of our traditions can offer needs continual correction and challenge. This is to help overcome blind spots (blind *sides*) as well as the tendencies to idolatry (the overidentification of our symbolizations of transcending truth with the reality of truth), to which all of our traditions are prone.

The following composite statement could be from either a man or a woman. This person is a Christian. Of course, we could have drawn an example from any one of many other traditions:

My faith has undergone some difficult changes in the past few years. Before, things had seemed clear. I knew who I was. I had my circle of friends, my work relations; I had a sense of the values and beliefs that were important to me and could tell you why they were important. I knew who God was and had a fair sense of how God fit into my life. But in recent years I have come through a time when things have gotten a bit messier.

Living with myself as an adult for twenty years or so, I have had to examine the dream with which I began. Some of it I have fulfilled, other parts of it I have given up—or had beaten out of me. Along the way, unexpected dimensions of me, and of life, have intruded into my earlier ways of seeing things. What previously seemed clear and unproblematic has become more complex, more mysterious, and strangely, more important to me. Let me try to put in words:

God seems to me now more mysterious than ever, yet somehow, more fundamentally important. God is subtle but profoundly real and powerful. I sense that God's way of working with us is more gradual and hidden than I once thought (or than I was taught). "Doing the will of God" for me now seems a much more *inductive* rather than a *deductive* process—and it *is* a *process!* The will of God is not some body of commandments or some demarcated path we are to find ready-marked through the wilderness. It is not, in any simple way, working to bring some clear conception of a "Kingdom of God."

Doing the will of God, I have come to believe, is something like creating a play together—actors working with a playwright-director. We improvise together in an overall plan that God has. The direction of that overall plan is what the "script"—the Bible—helps us to see. But our responses, our initiatives, our moves are important in this drama, as we try to shape our dance in relation to God's movements.

I have begun to understand in new ways that in Christ, God shows forth the divine purpose for *all* persons and nations. But paradoxically, this may not mean that all people have to come to know God in the way I, and we Christians, do. I believe that in Christ the character and purpose and love of God are made accessible to us in an unsurpassable way. Realizing this, and being committed to this, strangely, opens me to the possibility that the character, purpose, and love of God—who is truly universal —may be expressed also in the profound parts of other religious traditions.

This I know for sure: God is great as well as mysterious. Ultimately, all of us will find our destiny and fulfillment in God. God is the author and final determiner of history. We humans are called to a kind of partnership with God. And we need real redemption. For as Saint Paul put it, "The good we would do, we do not do, and the evil we would not do, we find ourselves doing. Who will save us from this strange mixture of life and death?"

Conjunctive faith combines deep, particular commitments with principled openness to the truths of other traditions. It combines loyalty to one's own primary communities of value and belief with loyalty to the reality of a community of communities. Persons of Conjunctive faith are not likely to be "true believers," in the sense of an undialectical, single-minded, uncritical devotion to a cause or ideology. They will not be protagonists in holy wars. They know that the line between the righteous and the sinners goes through the heart of each of us and our communities, rather than between us and them.

Universalizing Faith. The person or community of Conjunctive faith lives in paradox and in the tension of ironic consciousness and commitment. In an analogy with revolutionary theory, they can see the corruption and vulnerability of the old regime, even as they can also see and rejoice in the possibility of a new order, one more replete with a balance of equality and justice, of inclusion and corporate devotion to the common good. They recognize the imperative that all things be made new, yet they are deeply invested in the present order of things. They have attachments and commitments that make revolutionary alignment too costly and frightening to entertain. So they live divided in tension, working for amelioration and evolution toward justice, but deeply aware of their own implication in the unjust structures that they oppose.

The temptation of Conjunctive faith, thus, is to become immobilized in its compassion. The polarities in its loves and loyalties can seem to cancel each other. Persons of Conjunctive faith long for transforming newness; yet their integrity involves keeping steadfast commitments to institutions and persons in the present. They see the possibility, even the imperative, of lives lived in solidarity with *all* being. Yet their wills, affections, and actions manifest tension, splitness, and disunity. Being in but not of the world, they feel a cosmic homelessness and loneliness. For some, this longing and discomfort becomes the means by which they are called and lured into a transformed and transforming relation to the ultimate conditions of life—and to themselves and everyday existence with the neighbor. This transforming and transformed relation we call Universalizing faith.

The movement toward Universalizing faith is marked by the radical completion of two tendencies we have seen developing in the course of earlier stages. The first involves *decentration from self.* The radical decentration from self in Universalizing faith has several dimensions. The first is epistemological. We have seen in the description of development from one stage to another that each new stage brings a qualitative expansion in *perspective taking.* With each later stage, the circle of "those who count" in one's way of finding or giving meaning to life expands. From primal relations in intimate family, we gradually widen our circle of awareness and regard to extended family and friends, to those who share our political and/or religious identifications, and finally beyond those to humankind or Being, in an inclusive sense. Decentration from self in the epistemological sense means the gradual qualitative extension of the ability and readiness to balance one's own perspective with those others included in an expanding radius. It means "knowing" the world through the eyes and experiences of persons, classes, nationalities, and faiths quite different from one's own.

A second dimension of decentration that comes to a radical completion in Universalizing faith has to do with valuing and valuation. The developmental history of our devotion to values and centers of value parallels the course of decentration in our perspective taking. We invest in or commit to values that give our lives meaning and value. We "rest our hearts" on centers of value that confirm our identities and confer significance on our sense of selfhood. Put another way, we become attached to causes, persons, institutions, possessions, and the like precisely because they seem to promise to ground us in worth. Likewise, we tend to attach ourselves to certain appearances and promises of power. These sources of power, which promise to preserve our interests and values, help us deal with our fears and our insecurities as finite persons in a dangerous world of power. Across the stages of faith development, as the boundaries and identity of the self undergo clarification, each successive stage requires an expansion of the groups and interests whose valuing—based on *their* fears and anxieties about worth, significance, and survival—gradually become matters of our concern as well. This process reaches a kind of completion in Universalizing faith, for there a person decenters in the valuing process to such an extent that he/she participates in the valuing of the Creator and values other beings—and being—from a standpoint more nearly identified with the love of Creator for creatures than from the standpoint of a vulnerable, defensive, anxious creature.

From the paradoxical attachments and polar tensions of Conjuctive faith, the person best described by Universalizing faith has assented to a radical decentration from the self as a epistemological and valuational reference point for construing the world and has begun to manifest the fruits of a powerful kind of *kenosis* or emptying of self. Often described as "detachment" or "disinterestedness," the kenosis—literally, the "pouring out" or emptying of self described here—is actually the fruit of having one's affections powerfully drawn beyond the finite centers of value and power in our lives that promise meaning and security. "Perfect love casts out fear," as it says in I John 4:18. The transvaluation of values and the relinquishing of perishable sources of power that are part of the movement to Universalizing faith are the fruit of a person's total and pervasive response in love and trust to the radical love of God.

Let us listen to a voice representative of this stage and to the sacred text that guided the formation of this person's way of seeing and being:

There comes a time when an individual becomes irresistible and his action becomes all-pervasive in its effect. This comes when he reduces himself to zero.

For a nonviolent person, the whole world is one family. He will thus fear none, nor will others fear him.

It is no nonviolence if we merely love those that love us. It is nonviolence only when we love those that hate us. I know how difficult it is to follow this grand law of love. But are not all great and good things difficult to do? Love of the hater is the most difficult of all. But by the grace of God even this most difficult thing becomes easy to accomplish if we want to do it.

By detachment I mean that you must not worry whether the desired results follow from your action or not, so long as your motive is pure, your means correct. Really, it means that things will come right in the end if you take care of the means and leave the rest to him.

The last eighteen verses of the Second Chapter of the *Gita* give in a nutshell the secret of the art of living:

> . . . When you keep thinking about sense-objects
> Attachment comes. Attachment breeds desire,
> The lust of possession which, when thwarted,
> Burns to anger. Anger clouds the judgment
> And robs you of the power to learn from past
> Mistakes. Lost is the discriminative
> Faculty, and your life is utter waste.

But when you move amidst the world of sense
From both attachment and aversion freed,
There comes the peace in which all sorrows end,
And you live in the wisdom of the Self . . .

He is forever free who has broken
Out of the ego-cage of *I* and *mine*
To be united with the Lord of Love.
This is the supreme state. Attain thou this
And pass from death to immortality.

Love never claims, it ever gives. Love ever suffers, never resents, never revenges itself.

Have I that nonviolence of the brave in me? My death alone will show that. If someone killed me and I died with prayer for the assassin on my lips and God's remembrance and consciousness of His living presence in the sanctuary of my heart, then alone would I be said to have had the nonviolence of the brave.[10]

The foregoing quotes from the writings of Gandhi and from the *Bhagavad Gita* provide fitting expressions for Universalizing faith. I could have used examples from Buddhist, Christian, or Jewish sources and from a few honest humanist mystics and militants. Universalizing faith, in its authentic form, is recognizable in any culture or tradition. Despite differences in the metaphysical convictions and imagery used to express them and despite differences in their understandings of the relation of being and time, the quality of the lives of persons of Universalizing faith from whatever time or tradition are demonstrably similar in spirit and in power.

4. FAITH DEVELOPMENT THEORY AND THE HUMAN VOCATION

Now we must put the same questions to the faith development perspective that we have asked of the theories of Erikson, Levinson, and Gilligan. What normative image of adulthood comes to expression in this work? What vision of human wholeness and completion animates this research? When we ask faith development theory about the characteristics of the good man and the good woman, what portrait does it yield?

To answer these questions means to come to terms with a long-standing ambiguity in our work on faith development. It has been, on the whole, a fruitful ambiguity. But now is the time to try to clarify and move beyond it.

From a simple angle of vision one might answer the questions about faith development and the vocational ideal by pointing to the Universalizing stage of faith as providing the profile and characterization of this theory's image of human maturity. And that would not be entirely wrong. But it would not be entirely correct, either. Here is where we must face a central ambiguity: Does the Universalizing stage, with its radical transvaluation of valuing and its relinquishing of self as the epistemological and axiological reference for interpreting experience, truly constitute a normative image for *all* human becoming? Does a stage, attained by so few persons in any tradition and seeming to require the coupling of a strong mystical dimension with transforming social action qualify as representing a *general* vocational ideal?

Behind the doubts expressed in these questions, there lie issues that have been focused by several critics of our work.[11] First, there is the issue of the relative paucity of our data on persons of Universalizing faith. Second, there is the issue of the seemingly more radical transition between the last two stages of faith as opposed to the transitions between the earlier stages. And finally, there is the issue regarding the social feasibility or desirability of having very many persons of Universalizing faith around: Can one be of this stage and maintain intimate relationships? Can one be of this stage and contribute to the maintenance of complex social, economic, and political systems? Or put the other way around, can a stage that requires such decentering from self and detachment from material goods be representative of the callings of persons of a wide variety of temperaments, backgrounds, and worldviews?

Because of considerations such as these, Gabriel Moran and other sympathetic commentators on this work have suggested that Conjunctive faith be taken as the normative end point of the faith development sequence. As a stage, they suggest, Conjunctive faith meets the criteria for life in an interdependent, pluralistic global world. Moreover, they argue that to make this stage the culmination makes logical and empirical sense as having continuity with the progression of earlier stages. They observe that there is no radical disjuncture between Individuative-Reflective faith and Conjunctive faith, as there is between the latter and the Universalizing stage. Further, they suggest that because the Universalizing stage seems to require a religious, if not a theistic, orientation, it may in fact be *less* universal than the Conjunctive stage, which seems to involve no such necessity.

I find the foregoing considerations to be important. They have pressed me to try to penetrate and clarify the relationship of two factors in a person's development in faith—two factors that in theology have traditionally been identified as "nature" and "grace." With regard to these factors, the position of the critics that I summarized above could be stated in this way: The progression of stages from Primal faith to Conjunctive faith can be seen as descriptive of a *natural* process of development, with obvious parallels to processes documented in accounts of cognitive, moral judgment, psychosocial, and ego development. One need not advert to claims for the involvement of grace or revelation to account for a person's development, over time and in interaction with the conditions of existence, to the Conjunctive stage. Movement to the Universalizing stage, however, seems to require a disruption of or a disjunction from the "natural." Those persons who are best described by Universalizing faith seem to have undergone an experience of the negation of ties and affections that we generally take to be "natural." They seem to have undergone the negation of a kind of self-interestedness that also seems "natural." To be sure, the negation of these ties often turns out, in the end, to have been a *relativization* of them, with the relationships having been re-established but now with definite subordination of their value to the central value of the person's oneness with the Transcendent. Nonetheless, the motives, courage, and tranquility that make not only an assent but even a longing for this negation powerful in people seem to require an explanation based on the initiatives of the Transcendent—of Being, of God, or of Spirit. Such motives and longings seem to be the work of something like Grace.

My own position on these matters is the following: I believe that grace, as the presence and power of creative spirit working for human wholeness, is given and operative in creation from the beginning. In that sense, I agree with that theological tradition that argues that the "natural" or a "state of nature" are fictional concepts, corresponding to nothing in history or the present. Human development toward wholeness is, I believe, always the product of a certain *synergy* between human potentials, given in creation, and the presence and activity of Spirit as mediated through many channels. The most crucial factor differentiating the quality and movement of a person or group's development in faith, therefore, has to do with the conscious and unconscious availability of that person or group's potentials for partnership—for synergy—with Spirit. In a complex range of ways, we can be in either conscious or unconscious enmity with Spirit. From a variety of factors, the etiologies of which are exceedingly complex, we can bear deep dispositions that make us inimical to synergy with Spirit. Where and to the degree that we bear this kind of enmity, growth to and in the latter stages of faith will be blocked. When one who was previously blocked experiences the effective breakthrough of Spirit that brings release and new openness to synergy with Grace, we are in the presence of what Christian theologians have traditionally called "salvation" or "saving Grace." Christians have traditionally called the condition of enmity or blockage to synergy with Grace "sin."

The foregoing discussion provides a basis for moving beyond some of our previous ambiguities in characterizing the vocational ideal that comes to expression in faith development theory. The crucial point to be grasped is that the image of human completion or wholeness offered by faith development theory is not an estate to be attained or a stage to be realized. Rather, it is a way of being and moving, a way of being on pilgrimage. Faith is a relation of trust in and loyalty to one's neighbors, maintained through trust in and loyalty to a unifying image of the character of value and power in an ultimate environment. The human calling—which we take to be universal—is to undergo and participate in the widening inclusiveness of the circle of those who count as neighbor, from the narrowness of our familial beginnings toward real solidarity with a commonwealth of being. This calling means movement from the limiting love of those who love us and on whom we are dependent, toward the limitless love that comes from genuine identification with the Source and Center of all being. The faith development perspective depends on the conviction that each person or community continually experiences the availability of Spirit and its power for transformation. The patterns and causes of resistance to synergy with Spirit in growth toward wholeness need to be understood in a variety of ways, and they have to be worked with in a variety of ways. The goal, however, is not for everyone to reach the stage of Universalizing faith. Rather, it is for each person or group to open themselves, as radically as possible—within the structures of their present stage or transition—to synergy with Spirit. The dynamics of that openness—and the extraordinary openings that come occasionally with "saving Grace"—operate as lure and power toward ongoing growth in partnership with Spirit and in the direction of Universalizing faith.

NOTES

1. See especially James W. Fowler, *Stages of Faith: The Psychology of Human Development and the Quest for Meaning* (San Francisco: Harper & Row, 1981); and James Fowler and Sam Keen, *Life-Maps: Conversations on the Journey of Faith* (Waco, Tex.: Word Books, 1978).
2. Genesis 11:1–9.
3. For a description of our research procedures and interview protocol, see Fowler, *Stages of Faith*, pp. 307–312. See the forthcoming *Manual for Faith Development Research* (by James Fowler, Romney M. Moseley, and David Jarvis).
4. For a more detailed accounting of these stages, see Fowler, *Stages of Faith*, pp. 119–211.
5. Ulric Neisser, "The Development of Consciousness and the Acquisition of Skill," in P. M. Cole, D. L. Johnson, and F. S. Kessel, eds., *Self and Consciousness* (New York: Praeger, 1984).
6. Paul Tillich, *Systematic Theology*, vol. *I* (Chicago: University of Chicago Press, 1951) p. 191; and Paul Tillich, *The Courage to Be* (New Haven: Yale University Press, 1952), 57.

7. See Ana Marie Rizzuto, *The Birth of the Living God* (Chicago: University of Chicago Press, 1979).
8. In this and the following composite statements from other stages, I want to acknowledge the contributions of Mary Lou McCrary and Barbara Shuman, who conceived the idea of composite, representative statements and tried their hands at earlier versions. The composite statements used here, however, are by the author.
9. C. G. Jung, *Collected Works, vol. II, Psychology and Religion: West and East,* 2nd ed. (Princeton: Princeton University Press, 1969), pp. 287, 501, 369, 416, 419, et passim.
10. The quotes are from various writings of Gandhi selected and cited in Eknath Easwaran, *Gandhi the Man,* 2nd ed. (Petaluma, Calif.: Nilgiri Press, 1978), pp. 101, 105, 108, 115, 121–22.
11. For a balanced and insightful formulation of the criticism that follows and other critical insights, see Gabriel Moran, *Religious Education Development* (Minneapolis: Winston Press, 1983) pp. 107–136. Also see the forthcoming volume of critical essays on faith development theory edited by Barbara Wheeler, Sharon Parks and Craig Dykstra. Untitled, (Winona: St. Mary's Press, 1985).

IV. Adulthood, Vocation and the Christian Story

1. THE CHRISTIAN CLASSIC AND ITS NARRATIVE STRUCTURE

The previous two chapters have sought to present four developmental theories that offer us, in somewhat different ways, elaborated images of the human life cycle. In our consideration of these "myths of becoming," special attention has focused on the visions they offer us of the direction and shape of fulfillment in human becoming. We have treated these perspectives as pointers to images of human excellence and as sources of "vocational ideals." In choosing to present these developmental theories this way, I have meant to suggest that they, individually and as a group, have some important things to contribute to our moving beyond the present crisis of vocation and to working our way toward enriched and strengthened visions of human maturity. In a later chapter I intend to bring together some of the insights that seem particularly indispensable from these theories. In the meantime, however, I want to explore with you some normative perspectives on adulthood from a different kind of source.

Sociologist Daniel Bell, in *The Cultural Contradictions of Capitalism,*[1] makes an arresting case for his judgment that the secular sixties and the "me-generation" seventies would be followed by a resurgence of interest in and commitment to religion. Bell argues that "Modernism," as a dominant mood and sensibility in art, drama, film, literature, and music across the last 70 years, began as a prophetic and liberating "rage against (bourgeois) order." As such, it built on romanticism's insistence upon spontaneity and feelings as primal values and motives, adding to them the conviction that breaking the confining boundaries of convention leads to new *experiencing,* the only source of cultural newness and enrichment. Forfeiting criteria for assessing worth and truth in experience and becoming more frantic in its commitments to change, newness, and shock, Modernism, Bell contends, trivialized itself. Powerful in its iconoclasm and its work as cultural solvent, Modernism possesses no constructive principle. Irresistible in its unmasking of hidden pretensions and its disclosure of the chaos or murderousness concealed behind the facades of middle- and upper-class respectability, Modernism ends with the listlessness of *Waiting for Godot* or the hopelessness of *No Exit.* After a decade in which the promises of self-actualization and intentional narcissism coincided with the moral morasses of Vietnam and Watergate, it is not surprising that there should be, at present, a widespread search for moral bearings and spiritual depth.

Bell, like Paul Tillich before him, recognizes that any possibility of shared coherence of values and vision in a culture depends upon a vital religious center and its generation of living principles by which to honor the sanctity of the sacred. Religion, as Bell sees it, "is a constitutive part of man's consciousness: the cognitive search for the pattern of the 'general order' of existence; the affective need to establish rituals and to make such conceptions sacred; the primordial need for relatedness to some others, or to a set of meanings which will establish a transcendent response to the self; and the existential need to confront the finalities of suffering and death."[2]

Bell's recognition of the irreplaceability of religion in Modernity is welcome. His appreciation for the necessity of avoiding the abstraction of religious substance to ethical principles is insightful. His contention that the religious vitality that can sustain or renew cultural vision and values requires a living tension between the particular and the universal is correct. As a sometime reader of both men, I am struck by the linkages between Bell's analysis of our present social and cultural situation and the theological proposals, in recent years, of David Tracy. Bell describes Modernism as a "rage against order." David Tracy, drawing on the language of Wallace Stevens's poem, "The Idea of Order at Key West," entitles his first major book addressing these themes *Blessed Rage for Order*.[3] Tracy's second major book on these issues is *The Analogical Imagination*.[4] There, among other important themes, Tracy breaks new ground by offering a rich proposal for how particular religious traditions can offer their visional and ethical treasures in the context of radical pluralism, without falling into either a reductive demythologization or a defensive-assertive dogmatism. He offers us his discussion of the *religious classic*.[5] As a background for our consideration of the Christian story and vision —and of a Christian view of adulthood—Tracy's perspective is important.

Standing in the hermeneutical tradition of Hans Georg Gadamer, Tracy is concerned with the retrieval of tradition as a living vector in contemporary efforts to make meaning. Willing to take pluralism with radical seriousness, Tracy's aim is to clarify how elements from rich religious traditions can be offered to a cultural public without requiring the prior assent of faith, on the one hand, or falling into a nebulous abstraction, on the other. How can we offer the fertile substance of a particular religious tradition to persons of other—or no—traditions, without violating either the integrities of the tradition or of the publics whom our presentation addresses? Tracy's solution, following Gadamer, is the idea of the religious classic.

What is a "classic"? When we refer to a painting, a novel, an architectural structure, or a philosophical work as a classic, what do we mean by the term? When we designate a drama or film, a symphony or a sermon as a classic, what qualities do we have in mind? A classic is an expression of the human spirit that seems to gather into a fitting unity something that is fundamental, recurring, and universal in our experience. It brings into irresistible focus some perennial nexus or knot that, in every century, bedevils our species. Or it captures, in form and media that prove efficacious, year in and year out, some moment of sublime transcendence that again and again washes clear the gates of our perception. A classic stands the test of time. A classic brings to expression something that is fundamentally true about the human condition but does so in a way that respects the essential complexity, the stubborn persistence, and the honest opacity of its subject matter.

Honest opacity? Classics exhibit what some writers have called a "surplus of meaning." They exhaust our capacities for interpretation before we have exhausted their meanings. There is a penumbra of mystery around the heart of any true classic. It gives rise to conflicts of interpretation and discloses surprising depths as we inquire into its multiple layers of meaning.

The idea of a classic can be made clearer if we contrast it, as Tracy does, with the concept of a "period piece."[6] The latter, also an expression of the human spirit, captures something essential to a particular moment in our shared experience and brings it to clarifying expression with compelling effect. Period pieces can be extremely valuable, and, sometimes, they become classics. But usually the best-selling novel of this season is the cliché of the next, and the film that regaled everyone this summer is passé by fall. The designation *popular,* in addition to suggesting "lowbrow" (of the folk), often connotes something of the cut-flower character of the period piece.

The *religious* classic, in Tracy's usage, is a special instance of the larger idea of the classic. A religious classic, also an expression of the human spirit, has the special quality that it conserves and makes powerfully accessible moments that may be called "disclosure-concealment events." A religious tradition is constituted by a series of mutually interpreting, unified, and tensional events of disclosure-concealment of the kind that we call "revelation." Tracy speaks of revelation as the disclosure of the Whole by the power of the Whole. These moments of disclosure are also moments of concealment. God's self-disclosure never exhausts God's being, and our apprehensions and expressions of disclosure events are never adequate fully to appropriate what is offered. Again there is a surplus of meaning, an essential opacity, giving rise to conflicts of interpretation.

Against the backdrop of the idea of the religious classic, we turn now to consider the *Christian* classic.[7] My intent, in this introductory section, is to try to grasp, in holistic fashion, the essential *narrative structure* of the Christian classic. Once we have gotten a girth around its major movements, it will be possible to dig more deeply into those elements of a Christian view of the human calling that will enable us to bring them into critical and constructive dialogue with the previous psychological perspectives on adulthood.

One of the striking features of twentieth-century thought at every level is its appropriation of "process" as a fundamental or root metaphor for interpreting and managing our experiences. At every systems level and in every discipline, dynamism and process are king, and substance, stasis, and immutability have been dethroned. The dynamic character of narrative, as opposed to ontological categories inherited from preprocess metaphysical perspectives, is one of the reasons for the growing interest in theology as "story" and in explorations of the return to narrative as the primary mode of theological work. But the turn to narrative grows out of another critical reaction, this time to the philosophical expressions of processial thought itself. The language and imagery of process philosophy and theology have taken on highly abstract, formal modes of expression. The turn to narrative, therefore, reflects a fundamental need to reunite process with particular contents and contexts. It reflects a hunger to recover a sense of meanings as being connected with history, a sense of disclosure and depth as being connected with experience.

Alasdair MacIntyre's seminal book, *After Virtue*,[8] helps us see the critical and constructive role of narrative in the development of *paideia*[9]—the comprehensive approach a culture takes to the intentional formation of persons of virtue and strength in accordance with its visions of human excellence of being. MacIntyre contends that virtues, understood as moral strengths and habits, are defined and valued in relation to the particular "social *praxis*" of a given community or culture. The social praxis means, literally, the accepted and customary ways things are done in a society and the meanings attached to them. A given social praxis is legitimated and sacralized, MacIntyre suggests, by the shared mythopoetic "narrative structure" that gathers and grounds the world views, the beliefs, and the values of a people and culture.

Against the dual backdrops of our concern with visions of human excellence and our effort to clarify the narrative structure of the Christian classic, we are led to ask: What are the constituent elements of the Christian story and vision? What is the essential narrative structure of the Christian classic? Were we given the challenge faced by the first-century rabbi, Hillel, to tell the meaning of the law and the prophets while standing on one foot, how would we answer on behalf of the core meanings of the Christian master story?

My response to these questions must here be kept to the barest of outlines. In offering this skeletal overview, I acknowledge the stimulus I have received from theologian Gabriel Fackre's book, *The Christian Story*.[10] We can outline the major movements of the narrative structure of the Christian classic with reference to seven large chapters:

1. *God.* "In the beginning was the Word *(Logos),* and the Word was with God, and the Word was God . . ." (John 1:1). In the telling of the Christian core story, we cannot get behind this starting point. The principle of Being is Being itself. As a small boy I asked my minister father, after the manner of nine-year-olds, "Dad, if God created the world, then, uh, who created God?" Smug in my sense of brightness, I assumed no one else had ever thought to ask that question. After a pause, and with a look that conveyed infinite patience with my cognitive conceit, my father answered, "In the beginning was the Word . . . And the Word was God." At the time, I thought it was a cop-out. I have since learned that that is, indeed, where our story begins. And we learn that in that primal fellowship of Being, we are dealing with an inner-trinitarian fellowship, a threeness in oneness that already represented a profound unity in differentiation.

2. *Creation.* In the dynamic expression of Being, God gives being. *Ex nihilo,* out of and from nothing, from and by the Word, Being makes room for co-being. Being further differentiates itself, cleaves its unity, and sets free seeds of freedom and creativity potentiated with its own image. Generative loci of Logos are dispersed; the inner life of God makes room for expanded participation and partnership.

3. *Fall.* Finite freedom and vulnerability as well as the seeds of freedom, grow into the illusion (and the burden) of self-groundedness. Separated loci of Logos undertake to be primally creative, rather than participative. This results in breach, alienation, and enmity, between God and God's creation and between created beings. The image of God in the creature undergoes distortion and separation. Anxiety and the fear of nonbeing strengthen the desperate efforts to assert, establish, and protect the self. Communal and social structures, as well as the passions of finite hearts, reflect the defensive self-absorption of those who experience—without knowing what is missing—a sundering from the ground and source of Being. The separation is complete, in that there is no faculty, no organ, or no capacity of the finite being that is not marked by the consequences of alienation.

4. *Liberation and Covenant.* The triune God makes initiatives of reconciliation. God offers liberation (from bondage, from self-groundedness) and extends the call and imperative to reconciled partnership. God gives the gift of Way (Torah, Halakah, Law) that leads to righteousness. Then the narrative shows us a series of oscillations between covenant and falling away, covenant and falling away, covenant and falling away, with God consistently and redemptively manifesting *steadfast love and faithfulness (chesed)* until . . .

5. *Incarnation.* Logos becomes human, takes on flesh. God discloses in human being the erotic intention in creation. God shows forth the costly determination to restore *unity* between Creator and creature, and *com*munity between alienated and separated creatures. The intended already-but-not-yet char-

acter of God's promised universal commonwealth of love is instantiated in the tangibility of words, deeds, a broken and torn body, and a remarkable resurrection from the dead. The *cross* shows in double disclosure the depth of the divine love, on the one hand, and the power of evil in the defensive structures and resistance of human enmity toward God's future, on the other.

6. *Church.* Resurrection and the outpouring of Spirit from the resurrected Christ confirm and empower the Church in its calling to partnership with the redemptive and reconciling work of God in Christ and in its extension of the Christ's announcement of the in-breaking commonwealth of love. The Church is meant to proclaim and demonstrate the universal calling of humankind to covenant partnership in God's work in the world, in anticipation of the fulfillment of God's intended redemption of the world in just and righteous unity.

7. *Commonwealth of Love.* This is traditionally known as the "Kingdom of God." Coming to us from the future as the source of every present and of all pasts is God's future, the character of which—as a reign of inclusive righteousness and love—has been promised and disclosed in covenant and incarnation. This sovereign power of the future, the lure and imperative of the commonwealth of love, exerts its ultimately undefeatable power for newness, justice, and liberation-redemption. In the energy field released in the spirit of the risen Christ, and lured by the already-but-not-yet power of the commonwealth of love, we are called to be in and to call others to the vocation of partnership with God. This calling, this vocation, is the secret entrusted to faith, a secret we are mandated to disclose and proclaim in the power of the Spirit.

2. CHRISTIAN FAITH AND THE HUMAN VOCATION

Having given an account of the flow of the Christian classic's narrative structure, I turn now to the Christian understanding of the human vocation. In the spirit of offering access to a religious classic, I speak from within this tradition, inviting readers who may or may not share my commitment to it to enter into the perspective it offers on our calling, our nature, and our destiny as a species. To enter into this perspective requires no prior assent of faith, no prior option for this way of seeing and being in the world. It does not require the relinquishing or compromise of allegiances to another faith tradition. It is in the spirit of sharing a classic that one merely be willing to attend with care and to participate with sensitive imagination, postponing critical judgment until the initial sharing is ended.

Ancient Israel was constituted by the call of God—a people-forming, vocation-establishing call to a covenant relationship. Yahweh promised to keep steadfast faith with Israel and to make of them a nation of priests who would be partners in bringing about justice and righteousness on earth. Christians believe that in Jesus the Christ, the call of Israel came to be disclosed as universal and as pertaining to all people. We are constituted as a species and as persons by a call to covenant partnership with the one the ancient Israelites called "Yahweh." What sense can we make of this talk of "partnership with God"?

H. Richard Niebuhr, in teaching theology for thirty years at Yale Divinity School, developed a way of speaking about God's work in the world and the meaning of partnership in it that I still find extremely helpful. It involves the use of three major metaphors for illumining the character of the divine-human relation.[11] Niebuhr, of course, was well aware that he was employing metaphors, not speaking literally. A metaphor helps us understand the character or quality of an unknown or unfamiliar object by referring to it by reference to a known or more familiar object. For example, to say "My love is a graceful waterfall" is to employ a metaphor. The word *metaphor* comes from the Greek *meta* ("over") plus *phero* ("to carry") and means literally to "transfer" or "carry over" a meaning from one image or term to another. It is the nature of religious language to use metaphor for referring to divinity. It is the character of *biblical* language about the divine to use *multiple* metaphors for the divine-human relation. This is to avoid reification and idolatry. Further, the metaphors themselves are always *relational* in character. Biblical faith makes no claims to any knowing of God as God is in God's self (Kant's *"Ding an sich")*. The metaphors, symbols, and analogies employed in the biblical tradition represent God and humankind both in relation and taken together. They are metaphors of relation.

The first major metaphor that H. Richard Niebuhr employed is that of *God the Creator*. In this familiar image, Niebuhr asks us to see God as the source and center of all that has being and value. Radically, whatever *is* issues from God, and whatever has being has value because it issues from God. God the Creator is involved in ongoing works of creation. Creation is still happening. Less than a year ago I found myself in the Pacific Northwest and, for the first time, saw with my own eyes the crater and truncated peak that was Mount Saint Helens. As I gazed at the shattered matchsticks heaped on its mud-lava slopes, I heard the government geologist refer to it as "an adolescent volcano." And it struck me as never before that we live on a living planet. Creation, even on this globe, is not completed. And then, a short time later, I read of astronomers' discoveries of zones in our far-flung universe where even now, at astonishing temperatures and under terrific pressures, stars and planets are being formed and spun into space. The "maternity ward of the universe," the scientists called it. New creation, at the microcosmic level, came to visit us this Christmas when, on one of the coldest Christmas Eves in recorded history in Atlanta, we improvised a shelter for the three sheep and one she-donkey who made up the bestiary for the nativity scene at our local church. On Christmas morning, where there had been three sheep, there were now—miraculously and totally unexpectedly—four. God, the Creator: This is God's ongoing work of creation at every micro- and macrocosmic level. An ecological biologist, trained in the best hard-nosed research tradition, recently told me that he had decided after twenty years of struggle that it now seemed to him to take less effort to defend belief in a Creator than to give reasons for believing in randomness.

A second metaphor Niebuhr used refers to God's work of *Gov-*

ernance. In speaking of God as Governor, Niebuhr in no sense means for us to imagine in some anthropomorphic way an Oriental potentate sitting on a throne and swatting offenders with a scimitar. Rather, he means to refer to God's work of ordering and rectifying our common life. In this respect, Niebuhr invites us to think of God as a kind of *structure that intends righteousness in the processes of human history*. Martin Luther King, Jr. was close to Niebuhr's meaning, I believe, when he said, "The arc of history bends slowly, but it bends toward justice." Niebuhr's metaphor expresses his conviction that immanent in the processes of history there are structures that intend and bring about justice and righteousness. This is why corrupt and brutalizing regimes collapse as much from internal failure as from external resistance and counterforce. This is why societies and governments based on the economic foundations of slavery are inherently unstable and carry within them the seeds of their own destruction. To be sure, in order to see these structures-intending-righteousness that constitute God's governance, we have to think in terms of longer time spans than the three- to five-year plans by which most of us live our lives. At a crucial time in my young adulthood, I had an old Jewish friend. As a survivor of several pogroms and a refugee from several countries, he had built and lost four or five libraries and as many fortunes. He studied as a youth in Yeshiva Slobadka, in Odessa, with Rabbi Jacob Klausner. Sam had the disconcerting habit of thinking in terms of millennia. Despite his personal suffering and the horrible suffering of people of his kind, he could see—with prophetic vision—the structure-intending-righteousness in the processes of history. "We do not so much break the laws of God," said Paul Tillich," "as we break ourselves upon them."

Niebuhr's third major metaphor for God's work in the world is really a dual metaphor. He spoke and wrote of God as *Liberator-Redeemer*. Long before the current, recent interest in liberation theologies, Niebuhr invited us to envision God's work as liberation and redemption. He has in mind God's efforts, through a variety of overt and hidden means, to mitigate and overcome the consequences of our misused freedom. Each time I write or speak about this aspect of Niebuhr's theology, I remember a remarkable twelve-year-old boy I once interviewed in our faith development research. This lad grew up in an athiest family. In some ways it was a *militantly* athiest family. He had an older brother, age fifteen, who had a pet parrot that he had named "God." When the parrot squawked and made its grating parrot noises, the older brother, in order to infuriate his younger brother, shouted, "Shut up, God!" And the younger brother would become apoplectic in trying to defend the sanctity of the divine name. In this hostile environment, in short, this twelve-year-old had developed the most remarkably pure and strongly held theism I had ever encountered in a person of his age.

As I began to realize how clear and strong was this young man's commitment to God, I asked him, "What difference do you suppose it would make in the world if the God you believe in did not exist? How would it be a different world if God were not?" He paused thoughtfully for a few moments, and then he answered: "We can use the example of my fish tank, my aquarium. My aquarium is meant to be a perfectly balanced ecological system. The fish eat the plants and live on the oxygen the plants give off. The plants live on the waste from the fish and the carbon dioxide they put into the water. There are snails in the tank to keep the sides clean, and they live off the algae and the fish waste. So it is supposed to be a self-contained cycle, not requiring me to do anything." He continued, "But my aquarium is not perfect. Lots of times I have to do something to restore the balance. If I didn't, my fish would die." And then he looked squarely at me and said, "And we will never know how much God does every day to keep our world working as well as it does."

At the heart of God's redemptive and liberative work, Christians see the incarnation. This is the costliest expression of divine initiative and love and the paradigm event for seeing the everyday involvement of the Holy One in the redemption and liberation of persons and groups in bondage to alienation and self-groundedness, oppressed by hard social structures and the hardness of human hearts. In the Christian memory and hope, however, there are countless other images of liberation and redemption that also shape our perceptions and hope. These would include, most notably, the Exodus event—Israel's liberation from slavery in Egypt and election to covenant partnership.

In our brief consideration of these three major metaphors for the divine human relationship we have, so far, considered only half of the picture. You remember we indicated that biblical metaphors for God are always relational and never refer to the nature or essence of God apart from God's relatedness to creation and humanity. Each of these metaphors (or metaphorical clusters) that we have suggested has a correlated metaphor for human partnership in the work of God. If the major metaphors help us to begin to "see" God's work in the world, the correlated metaphors for human cooperation help us to grasp the ethical indicatives and imperatives of covenant partnership.

Think for a moment what that might mean: partnership in the Creative, the Governing, and the Liberative-Redemptive work of God. Of course, we will see that ultimately we are speaking of *one* unified work of God in the world—a work, albeit, of infinite complexity and scope. Therefore, the metaphorical correlates will overlap with each other at many points. But let's consider some of the meanings and substance of partnership through the lenses of each of these metaphors.

Partnership with God the Creator. This, indeed, means many things. Foundationally, it means participation in the procreative, nurturing process. Whether by biological parenting or by the investment of care in the children and youth of our common trust, it means being part of the treasuring of each child as a gift of God and of the nurturing of persons toward wholeness and richness of contribution to the common good. Partnership with God the Creator means being intentionally involved in the maintenance and extension of an ecology of care—an ecology of care for persons and for the environment. Care for the environment includes both care for the earth, including the quality of the physical environment—God's body—and also care for the environment of *spirit* —culture. Partnership with God the Creator includes (though it is not limited to) work in the arts and in the sciences, in technology and agriculture, in architecture and engineering, and in the medical arts and education. If the aim or goal of God's creative work is the fulfillment on earth of a commonwealth of love (traditionally the Kingdom of God), then the guiding impulse and criterion of cooperation with God's creative action is the vision of that commonwealth.

Partnership with the Governing Action of God. Because it takes the Fall seriously in its core story, any Christian understanding of partnership with God's governance must begin with recognizing the realism of restraint. This must include restraint at the level of individual selfishness and self-aggrandizement—beginning with parental restraint—but it must also include the necessary and legitimate restraint imposed by law and by the majesty and force of governments. God's governing work begins with and assumes the maintenance of good order, through just law, and through the ensurance of equality of life chances for all persons and groups. Cooperation with God's work of governance, under the criteria of the coming commonwealth of love, means endeavoring to make punishment restorative rather than punitive. It means, as Pope John Paul II recently wrote, "keeping capital in the service of labor" *(Laborens Exercens).* It means resistance to oppression and avoidance of revolution by changing revolting conditions. Crucial to grasping the spirit of partnership with the governing work of God is the recognition that it involves cooperation in restraint and rectification, in legislation and coercion, *under the impact and expectation of the in-breaking reign of God.* It believes, hopes, acts, and repents in the conviction that *God is active as a structure intending righteousness* in the complex contentions of limited perspectives and in the conflicts of interests between groups and between nations.

Partnership in the Liberative and Redemptive Action of God. It is important to remind ourselves at the outset that the central paradigm for human cooperation in the liberative and redemptive action of God is to be found in the *incarnation.* At the heart of the Christian understanding of incarnation is the reality of *Kenosis*— literally the self-emptying, the pouring out of self undertaken by

God in Jesus the Christ. This reminder warns us against triumphalist interpretations of human action in cooperation with the liberative-redemptive work of God. It also qualifies in a crucial way our images of human cooperation with the divine actions of creation and governance. One might read and think about partnership with the Creator and Governor with eyes shaped by images of *noblesse oblige*. One might think of human partnership with divine action in those two domains in terms of its supplying an additional superstructure of reward and sanction—adding theological legitimation to the recognition, deference, and material rewards that come from operating in high places. Not so. In any Christian understanding of the human vocation to partnership with God, all self- or class-aggrandizing images are undercut by the paradigm of the incarnation. God-creating and God-ruling are to be apprehended, Christianly, through the lenses of God emptying self, in radical love, to reclaim, restore, and rehabilitate persons and societies. Persons *may* occupy positions of prestige and material reward in partnership with God's creative and ruling action. However, these privileges and rewards are borne with detachment and generosity, carried as trusts in the service of the coming commonwealth of love.

Cooperation with the redemptive and liberative action of God *pervasively* qualifies a Christian understanding of our human calling. Centering in the paradigm of incarnation and, secondarily, in the Exodus event, it means construing partnership with God as always beginning in solidarity with God's love and passion for the fulfillment of creation and, therefore, in solidarity with God's passion for the release and reclaiming of those confined in bondage— the bondage of alienation and sin, the bondage of political and economic oppression. Solidarity with God's passion, in this double sense, means participating in God's *Kenosis*—God's giving of self, God's spending and being spent in the processes of liberation and redemption.

This entire thrust of the Christian understanding of the human vocation gives it, in the eyes of most of the world, a decidedly paradoxical character. Strength, in this perspective, requires a self-emptying that to the world looks like weakness. Leadership, in this perspective, involves the purity of motive required in servanthood. Fulfilling one's life means losing one's life in the costly expenditure of love. Wisdom, from this standpoint, means fixing one's navigational instruments on the promise and vision of a commonwealth of love, the contours of which—dimly visible to the eyes of the world—seem to be rank foolishness. Cooperation with the liberative and redemptive action of God, therefore, decisively shapes the ways persons seek positions, use resources, and make themselves available in the domains represented in the creative and governing action of God. Put most simply, it means an active, generative, initiating love for those whom God loves, which transvalues images of power, value, and success and which is ready to spend and be spent in God's work of fulfilling an inclusive commonwealth of love.

Christianly speaking, then, the human calling—the human vocation—is to partnership with God in God's work in the world. We humans, created in the image of God, are constituted by the address of God calling us to this partnership. God's calling into being constitutes each of us in our uniqueness and in our special purposes for living. It calls us into covenant relationship—a relationship of mutual trust in and loyalty to God and our neighbors. Please be clear about the fact that we are not referring here to a narrower idea, the idea of *Christian* vocation—a calling for followers of Christ alone. Rather, we are trying to bring to clarity a Christian understanding of the *human* vocation. What does it mean to be a mature human being? In what pursuit or devotion lies the fulfillment of human potentials? What is the shape of human completion and wholeness? Christian faith, in its classic story and vision, tells us that human fulfillment means to recognize that we are constituted by the address and calling of God and to respond so as to become partners in God's work in the world.

3. THE CHALLENGE OF VOCATION

In my efforts to clarify and renew an understanding of the human vocation, few teachers or thinkers have been more helpful to me than Walter Brueggemann. Theologian and Old Testament scholar, Brueggemann has written a number of decisive contributions in recent years. It was from his book *The Prophetic Imagination*[12] that I first learned, in a way that counted, that prophetic teaching and preaching do not begin with scolding or diatribes. Rather they begin with inviting people like ourselves—numbed with overstimulation and excessive demands or with defensiveness against our own inner accusations of moral failure—to begin to *feel* again. Prophetic teaching and preaching, he goes on to say, provide new energy and the gift of refreshing images by which to steer our lives and make sense of our callings.

For purposes of our present engagement, however, I want to refer to an article Brueggemann wrote in 1979 titled "Covenanting as Human Vocation."[13] In this article Brueggemann offers a number of memorable insights. To view humans as shaped for covenantal living, he says, "transposes all identity questions into vocational questions."[14] We move from the question Who am I? to the question *Whose* am I? We move from the question Who am I in relation to all these significant others in whose eyes I see myself reflected? to the question Who am I in relation to the Creator, Ruler, and Redeemer-Liberator of the universe? Eventually, from this perspective, all questions of identity become questions of vocation.

In ways that are resonant with our earlier discussion of the human calling to partnership with God, Brueggemann provides us with an arresting shorthand characterization of vocation: Vocation, he says, is finding "a purpose for being in the world that is related to the purposes of God."[15]

But even as we write and think about vocation here, I wonder if we really can reclaim this venerable and indispensable concept in its proper, powerful, and radical connotation. *Vocatio*—call, calling. In a memorable lecture, Carlyle Marney once asked, "How do we love God and love the neighbor?" And then he answered with Martin Luther's language, more than 450 years old now: "We serve God, we love God, we serve and love our neighbors *in commune per vocatione*—in community, through vocation."[16]

Reflect with me for a few moments about vocation in more

personal terms. In order to clean up and restore this powerful idea, we have to say some things about what vocation is not. First, vocation is *not* our job, our work, or our occupation. It may, of course, include our job, our work, or our occupation, but it should not be limited to the designation of one's source of livelihood. It is, therefore, a grave misuse of the term to speak about technical or job education as "vocational education." Second, vocation is not to be identified with profession. Admittedly, when we examine the rootage of the term *profession—professio*—which referred to the vows monks took as they established their vocations in the monastary,[17] and when we recognize that a profession involves putting knowledge and well-formed skills that use the self as their medium at the disposal of the needs of the community, we get much closer to the idea of vocation. But profession, in its contemporary usage—which is much closer to occupation—should not be taken as synonymous with vocation. Finally, vocation is not to be identified with career. It is not the trajectory of successes or failures or the sequence of jobs, professions, or occupations to which one has given oneself. Career *may* be expressive of vocation, but it is not necessarily identical with it.

Theologian Karl Barth, writing half a century ago, recognized this clearly. (In quoting him, I have found it necessary to leave his and his translators' consistent use of male pronouns unmodified.)

We speak of the vocation of man confronting and corresponding to the divine calling. It is clear that in so doing we give the term a meaning which transcends its customary use in the narrower, technical sense. Vocation in the usual sense means a particular position and function of a man in connection with the processes of human work, that is to say, his job; and then in the broader sense of a whole group of such positions and functions . . . . It is of a piece with the rather feverish modern over-estimation of work and the process of production that . . . it should be thought essential to man, or more precisely, to be the true nature of man, to have a vocation in this narrower sense of job or work. On such a view it is forgotten that there are children and the sick and the elderly and others for whom vocation, in this narrower sense of work can be only the object either of expectation and preparation, or of recollection. It is also forgotten that there are the unemployed, though these certainly are not without a vocation. Finally, it is forgotten that there are innumerable active women who do not have this kind of vocation.[18]

What *is* vocation then? I propose the following characterization: *Vocation is the response a person makes with his or her total self to the address of God and to the calling to partnership.* The shaping of vocation as total response of the self to the address of God involves the orchestration of our leisure, our relationships, our work, our private life, our public life, and of the resources we steward, so as to put it all at the disposal of God's purposes in the services of God and the neighbor. By *orchestration* I mean something like the artistry involved in blending the special qualities and range of a wide variety of musical instruments so that the resulting composite sound is beautiful and richer than the sum of its parts. Please understand that orchestration, in this sense, is not grim planning and studious, ascetic *control*—though in parts it may involve both. What I am trying to convey is more like the motion of dance, or the disciplined freedom of theatrical improvisation, or the responsive creativity of good conversation, in which the participants are really "all there."

Carlyle Marney, whose life and teachings influenced me deeply regarding vocation, had a gift for making complex things beautifully concrete. In the fifty-ninth year of his life (he died in 1978 at age sixty-one), he told a story from his childhood, close to the awakenings of his reflection on issues of vocation:[19]

Across nearly fifty years I recall the day the family voted to let Daisy go. Mama cried, we all cried, and Daddy offered to renege on her sale to the nice man who hoped to get just one heifer calf from his willingness to pay what Daisy cost thirteen years before. She had come to us as a heifer from Dr. Carr's locally famous herd of Blue Jerseys. She was temperamental, demanding, even truculent. Yet for all those years she gave the rivers of thick, creamy milk that supplied the Presbyterian manse, the Methodist parsonage, and our own icebox with an incredible four gallons of flavor per day.

But the same genetic miracle that made a Jersey give as much as a Holstein put Daisy in deep trouble every time she calved. She suffered terribly from mastitis. Groaning with pain from her swollen udders, the new milk locked in bulging mammaries, she would sink in her stall floor to die of fever on the very lip of a season's flood of lovely milk. Except— except for Mr. Adams' vocation.

President of our small town bank, he lived just across the alley in a wide, low house. Four A.M.; new calf in the stall; Daisy down on her knees; Mr. Adams with his bicycle pump and ointments and hot water under Daisy's big belly; my father with Daisy's tail over his shoulder, straining to keep her hindquarters from going down. While an amateur veterinarian, bank president, Presbyterian elder, neighbor, father pumped and oiled and soothed Daisy into production for another season. *This* is vocation!

Marney continues, with a set of questions and observations intended to clarify what I referred to above as the "orchestration" of one's roles, relations, gifts, limits, resources, and time:

But who is Mr. Adams? Was he neighbor, elder on a Christian mission, banker serving a very modest customer, or a cattle-loving veterinarian with a sympathy for a hurting beast whose name came from the side of a churn? Answer: He was all of these at once. But in the arrangement of the scenery of his life's drama, he was living out his identity, using the special gifts, interests, experiences that gave him a role as a means of relation. And his work, his energy in relation, were all serving a proper relational end. The term for the whole—role, work, proper end, is *vocation*. And from which of these roles and ends is his identity derived? Answer: From none of them. He is *all* of them at once.

But he is, on his knees, under the needy beast, in an *I-Thou* relation to his neighbor, and the cow, and the watching little boy holding a coal oil lantern on the whole vocational drama of salvation.

This story touches us and moves us with nostalgia for a simpler time than our own. It was a time when there was more stability in our communities, more continuity of relationships, and more opportunity, perhaps, for the appreciation and sharing of gifts with each other. Our society is more impersonal, our communities are much larger and more complex, and the challenges with which we need help are more baffling and intransigent than Daisy's periodic fevers. Moreover, the knowledge and skills required to contribute at relevant levels in the high specialization of our techno-economic systems make the issues of work and vocation exceedingly difficult in our time. I am convinced that Daniel Bell is right when he points to a major threefold division which is characteristic of advanced postindustrial societies—a division into the *techno-economic order,* the *polity* (or government), and *culture.* He illumines an important dimension of our crisis of vocational ideals when he argues that in contemporary society a major disjunction has been opened between culture—as the domain in which meanings and normative images of personhood are addressed-and the techno-economic order, where efficiency, profitability, and productivity tend to dominate and control the defining of virtues.[20] A central passion underlying this study is the concern, conceptually and ethically, to reunify the worlds of work, governance, and meaning. In the contemporary orchestration of our lives that vocation requires, we could do much worse than to work toward models of identity and vocation that stand in continuity with the rich and full life of Mr. Adams.

4. VOCATION VS. DESTINY, OR BEYOND SELF-ACTUALIZATION

The notion of vocation we are working with here becomes richer if we compare and contrast it with what I regard as its chief classical and modern rival in respect to vocational ideals. Here I have in mind the ancient idea of *destiny* and its contemporary counterpart, the idea of "self-actualization." As will become clear in the discussion that follows, I am drawing on sources that favor an interpretation of the idea of destiny as seen largely through the lenses of nineteenth-century romanticism. There is a more tragic understanding of destiny, deriving from Greek drama and mediated through ancient and modern stoic traditions, as well as contemporary existentialism, to which I will call attention in passing. But it is a particular modern blending of aspects of the ancient notion of destiny with the romanticism-inspired idea of self-actualization that I principally want to address.

I remember with some embarrassment during the thirtieth year of my life when, in my first year of teaching at Harvard Divinity School, I began to run low on material. In a kind of struggle for authenticity with the subject matter I was teaching, I began to share some autobiographical experiences with my students. I told them, blushingly, that early in my life I recognized that I had a sense of destiny such that I imaged the course of my life like certain advertisements used by the Shell Oil Company about fifteen years previously. Touting the virtues of a gasoline additive called "Platformate," which was supposed to increase pickup and power as well as extend gasoline mileage, the ads portrayed a graphic scene. On a wide desert road, two identical cars with equal amounts of gasoline drove side by side on a parallel course. But one of the cars, powered by Shell gasoline, had the benefits of Platformate. Quickly, the ad got to the point. Long after the first car, using ordinary gasoline, had choked to an ignominious stop, the Shell-powered vehicle burst through a highway-wide canvas sign a mile or two farther on, after which it continued on, with a cloud of dust, into the indefinite desert horizon. I told my students that I had felt, in that earlier period of my life, that I was going to burst through "average" like a gold Cadillac powered with Platformate. I was going to go far and go in class, carried by a sense of destiny—a sense of unique, special potential and of unique responsibility and burden.

In a book entitled *Personal Destinies,*[21] a philosopher named David Norton has offered us an interesting discussion of that idea of destiny that my confessional illustration meant to convey. Norton's book is based on the relation he claims to see between the ancient Greek idea of reliance on the inner voice of one's *daimon* for personal guidance and direction and the modern commitment to self-actualization. Norton subtitled his book *A Philosophy of Ethical Individualism,* and it is dedicated, with obvious admiration and gratitude, to the psychologist of self-actualization, Abraham Maslow.

"*Eudaimonism,*" writes Norton, "is the term for the ethical doctrine . . . that each person is obliged to know and live in truth to his or her *daimon,* thereby progressively actualizing an excellence that is his (*sic*) innately and potentially."[22] In referring to the image of the daimon, Norton reminds us of Socrates, the master of dialectical conversation, who would, from time to time, withdraw from the symposium, retire to privacy, and consult his own daimon, the voice of his own unique guiding spirit. Parallel with the Roman concept of the "genii," the "tutelary gods or the attendant spirits allotted to all persons as birth, determining the character and governing the fortune of each individual,"[23] the Greeks formed the equivalent idea of the daimon. For Norton, *Eudaimonism* means the happiness, fulfillment or state of well-being toward which one grows as one attends faithfully to the unique guiding voice of the personal daimon.

In his effort to recover this particular sense of destiny, Norton communicates a passionate belief that each person is special and potentiated with a unique possibility of singular excellence. His book has the worthy aim of trying to provide a historical and philosophical foundation from which contemporary individuals can offset their experiences of living in increasingly large, impersonal bureaucratic structures. He wants to counter the widespread effects of persons being identified by serial numbers in computer printouts, of mass education and media dullness, and the resignation with which large numbers in contemporary society settle into —or long to settle into—secure "niches" of bland routine. Norton has the admirable goal of calling persons to specialness and excellence on the basis of his appeal to the *daimon,* the inner voice of the soul. He offers us one very memorable image I would like to share:

In pre-Hellenic Greece, sculptors made busts of the semi-deity Silenus that had a trick to them. Inside the hollow clay likeness was hidden a golden figurine, to be revealed when the bust was broken open. Toward the conclusion of Plato's *Symposium,* Alcibiades says that Socrates is akin to a bust of Silenus. On the outside he is bald and pot-bellied, and he clothes his thoughts in earthy language; but he who can perceive the Socrates within the clay will cast his eyes on "the most divine." This episode means much more than would a testimonial to the uniqueness of Socrates, made by a drunken Alcibiades. It is a testimonial to the exceptionality of Socrates that makes use of the fundamental Greek conception of personhood. To the Greek understanding not Socrates alone, but every person is a bust of Silenus inevitably in some degree flawed and misshapen in appearance, but containing inside a golden figurine—one's daimon.[24]

Norton's message, elaborated and reiterated in his book, can be reported in his own summary: "Each person is a bust of Silenus containing a golden figurine, his daimon. The person's daimon is an ideal of perfection—unique, individual and self-identical."[25] The ethical imperative of *Eudaimonism,* which Norton is willing to equate with "self-actualization," calls for a person courageously, steadfastly, and undistractedly to attend to the innately given potentiated excellence (*areté*) seated in her/his daimon. The committed actualization of that excellence, under the adversities and challenges of historical existence, results in the enactment of a person's singular, unique destiny.

Every person is both his empirical actuality and his ideal possibility, or daimon. Connecting the two is a path of implications, whose progressive explication constitutes what the Greeks termed the person's "destiny" (*eimarmene,* deriving from the archaic *moira,* or "fate," and representing the interiorization within man of what had earlier been thought to be imposed upon him from the heavens). According to self-actualization ethics it is every person's primary responsibility first to discover the daimon within him and thereafter to live in accordance with it. Because perfection is incompatible with the conditions of existence, one's daimon can never be fully actualized in the world, but by living in truth to it one's unique perfection can be progressively approached, and such endeavor manifests in the world one's excellence or *arete*—an objective value.[26]

Our contemporary philosophers and psychologists of self-actualization and Eudaimonism say to us, "Break open the crust of that socially constructed persona, or set roles, that define your life. Discover the gold figurine of your daimon, and make the single passion of your life the realization of your unique and special excellence." They call us to heroic and disciplined pursuit of this internal truth, and they promise us the deep satisfaction that comes with the sense of authenticity and the achievement of excellence. Rollo May, in a book entitled *Freedom and Destiny*,[27] presents the more sober notion of destiny that I earlier identified with the Greek tragedians and the Stoics (and contemporary existentialists). May, in a richly textured discussion, says that destiny is that combination of talents and gifts we are given as persons, taken together with the limits deriving from our biological endowments, our economic and social conditions, and our relational and spiritual environments. Freedom arises, says May, as we honestly and courageously face our destiny with its limits and decide what we will do to transform it for usefulness and self-fulfillment. Whereas for Norton destiny is promise and unique potential, for May it is the horizon of possibilities and limits that we are dealt, which constitute the "givens" with which we must contend as we try to make something of our lives.

In light of our earlier consideration of a Christian view of the human vocation, let us now reflect on some of the implications of this discussion of Eudaimonism, destiny, and self-actualization. Both of these views of destiny, whether the optimistic innatism of Norton or the stoic existentialism of May, center on a heroic view of the self. Fulfillment of the self depends almost entirely on the resourcefulness, courage, and resoluteness of the actor. In the one case, this involves wholehearted commitment to attending to the guidance of one's daimon; in the other, it means a clear-eyed facing of the balance of possibilities and limits imposed by one's endowments and by the constraints and supports of one's environment. In both cases, the heroism is of a distinctly individualistic sort. One realizes one's destiny in opposition to or in spite of others. At best, it seems, one can help others by being an example of integrity and self-responsibility. Norton writes: "Eudaimonism teaches that the supreme help a man gives to others subsists *in* his integrity and self-responsibility, and cannot be predicated upon the ruin of these."[28]

Both of these versions of destiny and self-actualization lead toward what may be our most serious modern heresy, the individualistic assumption that we are or can be *self-grounded persons.* This assumption means believing that we have within us—and are totally responsible for generating from within us—all the resources out of which to create a fulfilled and self-actualized life. It is in contrast to this enticing, but finally illusory, strategy that I want to return to our discussion of the Christian vision of the human vocation. I want to suggest that vocation, seen as a call to partnership with God on behalf of the neighbor, constitutes a far more fruitful way to look at the question of our specialness, our giftedness, and our possibilities of excellence.

The Christian view of vocation sees everything that the notion of destiny does. It affirms the specialness and uniqueness of each of us. It calls us to excellence and occasionally to self-sacrifice requiring extraordinary courage and commitment. To be in vocation calls us to stringent disciplines and to certain kinds of asceticism. But in all these affirmations and callings to a strenuous investment of self, the fundamental motives and strategies of vocation are different from those of the strategies of the realization of one's destiny. In the latter—the pursuit of one's destiny—self-fulfillment and the work of self-actualization constitute the prime reason for living and the goal of all striving. The strategy of fulfillment calls for a direct assault upon the citadel of "goodies." It means maximizing one's accumulation of those qualities and goods that promise to guarantee one's fullness and completion. And, paradoxically, as Daniel Yankelovich has seen so clearly, this very strategy of pursuit alienates us from the bonds of community and intimacy, and from commitments to causes whose worth transcends our own, upon which true fulfillment depends.[29]

From the standpoint of a Christian view of the human vocation, the Eudaimonist's "golden figurine within" is inevitably an idol. In the perspective of vocation, we are called to personhood in relationships. There is no personal fulfillment that is not part of a communal fulfillment. We find ourselves by giving ourselves. We become larger persons by devoting ourselves to the pursuit of a common good. From the standpoint of vocation, fulfillment, self-actualization, and excellence of being are by-products of covenant faithfulness and action in the service of God and the neighbor. Rather than the golden figurine within, Christians see our potential as humans to be represented, as it says in Ephesians 4:13, "in a mature personhood that partakes of the measure of the stature which belongs to the fullness of Jesus Christ." That's the secret of our potential; that's the goal of our development. It is gift; it is by-product of faithful response to the faithful love of God.

Let me point out to you some of the consequences of understanding our lives in terms of vocation. First, in vocation we are called to an excellence that is not based upon competition with others. In vocation we are called to realize excellence as a result of God's addressing us but not with the motive of outstripping others. God has called each of us, with our unique range of gifts and our unique patterns of limits, and calls us to a vocational adventure that is distinct from that of anyone else. We do not need to establish it in competition with others.

Second, this understanding of vocation frees us from anxiety about whether someone else will fulfill our particular destiny before we get there or whether someone else will beat us to that singular achievement that would have justified our lives. If we are faithful in the relation to God and neighbors that is our vocational pilgrimage, that worry can take care of itself. There are a vast number of opportunities for partnership in God's work in the world; there is no shortage of significant ways to be part of the divine action.

Third, to be in vocation frees us to rejoice in the gifts and graces of others. In vocation we are augmented by others' talents rather than being diminished or threatened by them. In vocation we rejoice to be part of an "ecology of giftedness" in which a complementary division of labor frees and empowers persons to contribute to the common good at their points of strength.

In the fourth place, freed from jealousy and envy, able to celebrate the gifts of others, we are freed from the sense of having to be all things to all people. In vocation we are freed to do well those things that are intrinsic to our callings. At the same time we are freed from either the inflation of trying to be Godlike in super- or omni-competence or the deflation that inevitably comes when we fail and find our limits. In vocation we can experience our *limits* as gracious, even as we can experience our gifts as gracious. In vocation our responsibility, though vast, is finally limited. Our partnership—with God and with other covenanted ones—is finally a limited-liability partnership, because God is sovereign.

Fifth, in vocation we are called and freed to seek a responsible balance in the investment of our time and energy. Vocation is the opposite of workaholism. Traditional Lutheran ethics spoke of the "orders of creation," the areas of family, education or culture, economy, government, and church. Vocation means a pattern of faithfulness in appropriate participation in each of these areas. The degree and intensity of involvement in some of them will vary with the age and stage of our lives or with the particular shape of our calling. But freed from the need to ground or vindicate our own worth, in vocation we need not overbalance our self-giving in one or another of these areas.

Sixth, in vocation there is an important sense in which we are freed from the tyranny of time. If I have to realize the golden statue within me and if I must accomplish this in finite time in order to justify my having lived, then time becomes my enemy. Time becomes an ever-receding commodity, scarcer and scarcer, and I become more and more intense about making time serve my particular needs. Vocation, on the other hand, says that we are called into time; we are given life. In fidelity we understand that we are also given death, whenever it comes. When we are in vocation, time is our friend. Anne R. Mayeaux, one of my associates at the Center for Faith Development, has helped me understand that a life trajectory lived in vocation reveals, in whatever fraction of that life we are given to live or to see in others, the integrity of the whole.

Finally, we need to link our discussion of vocation to our earlier consideration of adult development. We need to see vocation as dynamic, as changing its focus and pattern over time, while continuing as a constant, intensifying calling. At this point we should remember Daniel Levinson's idea of the evolving individual life structure. As we saw in Chapter II, Levinson means by this idea the evolving and changing pattern of relationships to persons, to institutions, and to causes that characterize our lives at any given time—the configuration of our interchanges with the world, the pattern of our leisure, our faith, our public and private lives. Our life structures change and evolve over time. As we move from one season of our lives to another, in kaleidoscopic fashion the configurations that are our life structures alter in shape and complexity. A Christian view of the human vocation suggests that partnership with the action of God may be the single most fruitful way of finding a principle to orchestrate our changing adult life structures.

NOTES

1. Daniel Bell, *The Cultural Contradictions of Capitalism* (New York: Basic Books, 1978), pp. xx–xxi, 146–171.
2. Ibid., p. 169.
3. David Tracy, *Blessed Rage for Order* (New York: Crossroad-Seabury Books, 1975).
4. David Tracy, *The Analogical Imagination* (New York: Crossroad, 1981).
5. Ibid., chaps. 3–5.
6. David Tracy, public lectures, Boston College, Summer 1979.
7. For Tracy's discussion, see David Tracy, *Analogical Imagination,* chaps. 6–7.
8. Alasdair MacIntyre, *After Virtue* (Notre Dame: University of Notre Dame Press, 1981), p. 15.
9. See Werner Jaeger's massive 3-volume work, *Paideia: The Ideals of Greek Culture,* trans. Gilbert Highet (New York: Oxford University Press, 1939–1944).
10. Gabriel Fackre, *The Christian Story* (Grand Rapids, Mich.: Eerdmans, 1978). My discussion differs from that of Fackre in a great many ways, however.
11. For an elaboration of Niebuhr's use of these metaphors in his lecture courses at Yale, see James W. Fowler, *To See The Kingdom: The Theological Vision of H. Richard Niebuhr* (Nashville, Tenn.: Abingdon Press, 1974), chap. 3.
12. Walter Brueggemann, *The Prophetic Imagination* (Philadelphia: Fortress Press, 1978).
13. Walter Brueggemann, "Covenanting as Human Vocation," *Interpretation* 33 (2): 115–129.
14. Ibid., p. 125.
15. Ibid., p. 126.
16. Carlyle Marney, "How to Be a Human Being" (recorded tape) (Nashville: Broadman Press, 1976).
17. Dennis M. Campbell, *Doctors, Lawyers, Ministers* (Nashville, Tenn.: Abingdon Press, 1982), p. 18.
18. Karl Barth, *Church Dogmatics,* Vol. III:4 (Edinburgh, Scotland: T & T Clark, 1961), p. 599.
19. Marney, "How to Be a Human Being."
20. Bell, *The Cultural Contradictions of Capitalism,* pp. 3–30.

21. David Norton, *Personal Destinies: A Philosophy of Ethical Individualism* (Princeton: Princeton University Press, 1976).
22. Ibid., p. ix.
23. Ibid.
24. Ibid., pp. 5–6.
25. Ibid., p. 14.
26. Ibid., p. 16.
27. Rollo May, *Freedom and Destiny* (New York: Norton, 1981).
28. Norton, *Personal Destinies,* p. 14.
29. Daniel Yankelovich, *New Rules: Searching for Self-Fulfillment in a World Turned Upside Down* (New York: Random House, 1981), chaps. 3–5.

V. Christian Community and Adulthood

1. SELF AND OTHERS: FROM DESTINY TO VOCATION

Several years ago a colleague of mine made an arresting statement. He said, "There are two kinds of persons in educational institutions: those that serve the institution, and those that make the institution serve them." Circumstances in which we both were involved at the time made me reflect on the implications of his statement for my self-understanding. I have not forgotten the statement, however, and as I am reflecting on questions of vocation and destiny now, it seems clear to me that my colleague's typology is too simple. In light of the previous chapter's discussion of these two concepts, it seems that we might enrich his typology in ways that could be useful in the effort to clarify the dynamics of transformation from self-groundedness to vocation and from adulthood to Christian adulthood.

As a summary of motives and orientations toward the institutions and communities in which we serve, consider the following matrix:

destiny	A. Those who serve the institution (for self)	B. Those who make the institution serve them (for self)
vocation	C. Those who serve the institution (for vocation)	D. Those who make the institution serve them (for vocation)

Undoubtedly, this too is excessively simple. It does have the virtue, however, of clarifying and focusing for us several sets of crucial issues we must face as we draw together and deepen the insights offered us by adult developmental theories and the Christian vision of the human vocation. For example, my friend's simpler model failed to see that there are those who, seemingly with devotion and self-sacrifice, serve the institution primarily for the sake of being supported, protected, validated, or justified by it. These persons (position A) represent the kind of belief in self-groundedness that destiny involves, only they do not trust enough in their own projects or abilities confidently to require the institution to accommodate to their interests. So they elect the institution's project—or some part of it—as their own, and their colleagues and others involved in the community of the institution perceive them to be selflessly devoted to the common good. It is not surprising, however, that at some hidden or unconscious depth, these persons feel resentment when the institution fails to recognize the sacrifice they have made and anger when they feel the gap or vacuum that has resulted from their alienation of the pursuit of their own projects. Similarly, my friend's typology failed to recognize that there may be those (position D) who indeed succeed in making the institution serve their projects but do so not primarily for purposes of self-aggrandizement. Rather, the power of their responses to their own callings and the exercising of their gifts have succeeded in impacting the institution's priorities and in helping to determine the institution's collective sense of mission. Others in the community have responded to their vocations and have recognized them as essential to what the institution itself is called to be and do.

The typology of motivations introduced above can be expanded and extended to other areas of our lives than educational institutions. In public life and private life, in areas of work, profession, and the family, in religious communities and voluntary agencies, our chief motives for service are likely to fall more into one of these four positions than the others. There is little reason to assume that we are consistent in the pattern of our motivations as we move from one domain to another. The real problem is, however, that the structure of our motives and the wellsprings of our service are seldom clear either to us or to others. Positions A and C, both involving the subordination of self to institution—or of self to collectivity—can look very much alike. It takes several months or years of sustained observation to identify which of these positions most accurately and consistently characterizes the behavior of an associate or colleague. And it takes years to be clear about our own motives in this regard. Similarly, positions B and D have a great deal in common in terms of the way they look to other people and feel to ourselves. There is likely no area of potential self-knowledge where we are more subject to self-deception and more tempted to resort to self-serving rationalizations than in accounting for our efforts to influence and determine the social collectivities of which we are a part and the lives of those involved in them. Likewise, there are few areas in which it matters more to us that we create a good impression on others than regarding the motives for our claims for special privilege, for unusual institutional or moral leeway, or for their respect.

Two axes underlie this matrix of motivation: One I will call, following David Bakan, the axis of *agency* and *communion*.[1] The other I will call, following Walter Brueggemann, the axis of *self-groundedness* and *covenant*.[2] These are not new themes to our discussion, of course, but drawing them together in this way enables us to see what is at stake in any consideration of transformation from a dominant orientation to a sense of destiny to a dominant orientation committed to vocation. Agency and communion represent a true polarity in our social existence. We know we are dealing with a true polarity when we cannot think of one side of a conceptual pair without depending, in our thinking, upon the other. Paul Tillich speaks of "the courage to be a *part*" (to participate, to belong, to be intimate) and indicates that it exists in polar tension with "the courage to be *apart*" (to stand alone, to take responsibility for the self).[3] This polarity shows up in the destiny-vocation matrix in our realization that the person best described by position A is also, to some degree, accomplishing the goals of position B. A parallel statement can be with regard to positions C and D. Whether we approach our lives in terms of destiny or vocation, there must be some reciprocity between *agency,* the initiatives and interests of the self, and *communion,* the subordination of self-interest to the welfare and good of the collectivity.

It is not so clear at first glance that the other axis involved in our matrix represents a polarity—the axis of self-*groundedness* and *covenant.* The linkage between them and the factor that holds them in polar tension becomes visible when we realize that both orientations are forms of faith. Both involve the placing of our deepest trusts and loyalties. In self-groundedness, our deepest trusts and loyalties are invested in the resources, the potentials, and the powers at the command of the self. Relationships, our memberships in collectivities, the roles we play, our gifts and talents, and the powers of institutions with which we are involved all become *instrumental* when self-groundedness dominates the placement of our trusts and loyalties. All of these must be made to serve the survival, security, and significance of the self and its world. They must establish, vindicate, and perpetuate our worth; they must contribute to and sustain a structure of meaning that keeps the self—and the extensions of self in relations, possessions, and accomplishments—central.

In covenant existence, on the other hand, trust and loyalty are invested in a triadic pattern. Covenant existence acknowledges life as gift and trust—from other persons and from a Creator.[4] It accepts the fact that worth and significance are conferred and that justification and vindication come with being. It knows and accepts that it is welcomed into a structure of meaning that includes its own potential and contribution but that these are joined with those of others in a larger tapestry of purpose and intentionality. Relationships, memberships, roles, talents, and gifts, therefore, are not merely instrumental in the vindication of the self. Rather, they are trusts that one is uniquely freed and empowered to develop and enjoy but that one is also committed, in fidelity and gratitude, to exercise on behalf of the common good.

To the degree that destiny involves commitment to self-groundedness, it skews the axis of agency and communion. Agency must dominate and communion must be subordinated, however, subtly or blatantly, to the actualization of the self. To the degree that vocational existence involves commitment to covenant, it restores the balance of agency and communion. It frees one to be a self in community, without manipulating or controlling others for the sake of vindicating the self. And it empowers one to contribute to the furthering of causes and meanings that transcend the self in importance and to embrace the risks to self that such commitments require.

As I complete this book, Atlanta mourns the death of Benjamin E. Mays, president emeritus of Morehouse College and chairman emeritus of the Atlanta school board. At the age of ninety, Dr. Mays looked back on a life notable for much more than longevity. An extraordinary group of young to middle-aged men and women, black and white, leaders in politics, business, education, and the arts, testified to the powerful impression upon them of his spirit, integrity, and unswerving commitment to excellence. The college he directed for twenty-eight years takes its place among the premier institutions of higher education in the country. An urban school system that had to address the critical issues of desegregation and middle-class flight from the public schools has survived with growing stability, quality, and tangible promise of excellence. Mays could have taken positions that would have given him visibility and opportunities to serve in Philadelphia or Geneva, Switzerland, and many other places. He "elected"—as he put it—to invest himself in the South. "This region was down so far," he said, "that I wanted to be part of its recovery and its achievement of greatness. I wanted to be part of building a New South."

Dr. Mays was *not* a self-made man. Because of his promise as a child, because of his willingness and readiness to learn, he was given the very best opportunities and support a people poor in material resources but rich in faith, determination, and vision could offer. It is as though his life, committed from a young age to the service of God and his people, became a center around which Spirit gathered itself so that through trials and struggles, through dark nights and sunlit horizons, his presence became the occasion

for redemptive and empowering energy, for reconciling and transforming power. Those who knew Dr. Mays testify, without senti-
mentality or the mawkish cant of pseudo-celebrity, to the trans-
parent goodness of the man, to his self-emptying commitment to
the welfare of others, and to the contagion of his joy and his belief
in the present possibility of a new world of justice and peace.

In strange ways, the truths of an otherwise puzzling New Testament passage begin to come clear in light of our consideration of
the destiny-vocation matrix and the life of Benjamin E. Mays. I
refer to the saying attributed to Jesus in all three of the synoptic
gospels (and twice in Matthew and Luke): "Therefore take care
how you listen; for whoever has, to him shall *more* be given; and
whoever does not have, even what he thinks he has shall be taken
away from him" (Luke 8:18. See also Matthew 13:12; 25:29; Mark
4:25; and Luke 19:26). Its meaning, otherwise obscure and strange,
points to the multiplication of fruits and goodness that come with
the grateful receipt and generous use of the gifts (*charismata*) that
God provides. The hard saying about the one who "does not
have" refers, I believe, to the person (institution, corporation, nation) who does not acknowledge gifts with gratitude and expend
them in the service of the common good but rather sets about
shoring up, defending, and claiming special prerogatives for the
self on the basis of the gifts. ". . .(E)ven what he thinks he has
shall be taken away from him."

Destiny, founded on the claim or the despair of self-groundedness, implies individualism. Vocation, grounded on the triadic
faithfulness of covenant, implies community. We turn now to
consider the priority, in vocational existence, of community.

2. VOCATIONAL EXISTENCE AND CHRISTIAN COMMUNITY

Among other things, the previous section has brought to our
attention the ambiguity of our motivations for service and excellence, as well as the possibilities for self-deception inherent in both
a sense of destiny and a conviction of calling. Implicit in our con-

siderations there was the recognition that both a sense of destiny and a conviction of vocation can be sources of institutional and/or political, economic, and social power. Associated with power there are, inevitably, potentials for the corruptions attendant on both the conditions of unaccountable powerfulness and unmitigated powerlessness. Further, there are the potentials for jealousy, division, resentment, competition, hatred, violent assaults on character and life, and the terrible wastage of human energy and passion on internecine power struggles.

The political and economic tradition that C. B. Macpherson has called "possessive individualism"[5] (Hobbes, Locke, and Adam Smith) has sought to solve the problems mentioned in the previous paragraph by considering each of us to be a "tub that sits on its own bottom," in terms of work, the acquisition of property, and self-sufficiency. The solution to our competitiveness, our inequality of gifts, and our dangers to each other, in this tradition, lies in the forming of compacts or contractual societies. In such societies, each of us alienates a certain measure of our freedom and authority and invests it in the authority of a sovereign or a ruling body, who, it is trusted, will govern to protect the rights and serve the interest that all members have in security and peace. The political philosophy of possessive individualism seeks to maximize the freedom of each individual to pursue his/her conception of the good, while providing enough restraint of human enmity and destructiveness to provide security for this process and its results.

To speak of community (even the contractarian community of possessive individualism) as a "solution" is already to betray our tendency to forget that we are fundamentally social creatures. There is no selfhood apart from community; no faith apart from community; no destiny and no vocation apart from community. A community that centers its hopes and expectations for human excellence and contribution in the concept of vocation, however, is very different from the contractual society, with its "thin theory of the good," envisioned by the Hobbes-Locke-Smith tradition. To see this, we must move from contract to covenant, and from a minimalist conception of rights to a shared vision of a quality of life that fulfills God's intention for a commonwealth of love on this earth. For the awakening, nurture, affirmation, and ongoing accountability of vocation, we must look to communities of faith. No account of how communities awaken and support vocation will be adequate, however, unless it enables us to come to terms with the ambiguities of destiny and vocation, as well as the corruptions of power and powerlessness to which they can give rise.

The community of faith I want to discuss is the one formed around Jesus as the Christ. This is the community that shaped its identity under the impact of Christ's life, death, and resurrection, employing the enormous energy that came with the gift and powerful presence of Christ's Spirit. Continuing in the spirit of sharing a classic, which we introduced in Chapter IV, I will speak from *within* the Christian community, trying to give a version of its self-understanding, its horizon of meanings, and its sense of corporate and personal mission that has integrity. The structural and dynamic features supporting the Christian community's conception of the human vocation, however, are applicable to other communities of faith as well, as I shall try to illustrate later.

There are five interrelated, integrated, but analytically separable levels of meaning and orientation by which communities of faith form persons and groups for vocational existence. While I shall discuss these five levels from the standpoint of Christian faith and community, I invite readers to test their applicability with reference to other traditions as well.

1. The provision and instantiation of a *shared core story*. To awaken and inform—and to hold accountable—the vocations of its members, a community of faith must shape its identity in relation to a corporately held narrative structure. This involves an account, as I suggested in Chapter IV, of the history and pattern of God's relation to creation and the moments of disclosure-concealment when God initiated reconciliation and renewed the possibility of human partnership. As we shall see in more detail in a moment, two important vectors of vocational identity take form in the creative

and transformative interplay between one's personal narrative and the core story of a religious tradition.

2. A participation in and life-prioritizing identification with the
central passion of the shared core narrative. As will have to be
made clearer later, the central passion of the Christian core
story focuses in Jesus's preaching and embodiment of the in-
breaking, already-but-not-yet commonwealth of love and in
his suffering and death by which the redemption and reconciliation necessary for the Kingdom were decisively begun.
Christian vocation awakens and forms as persons enter into
and find a purpose for their lives *in relation to this double sense
of the passion of Christ.*

3. A formation of the *affections*—a person's deep and guiding
emotions, the wellsprings of motivation in a person—in
accordance with the community's identification with its central passion. Called variously "fruits of the spirit" and "gracious affections," these qualities of personhood, these deep
dispositions of the heart, are by-products and results of persons' responsiveness to the love and action of God.

4. The generation of *virtues*—moral strengths and actional skills
that become consistent, constituent dimensions of personal
and corporate action. These are strengths of perception,
judgment, and action that serve the central passion of the
community of faith and give tensile character to the affections.

5. The *practical and particular shape of worldly vocation* in each life
in the community and their interrelatedness in mission and
mutual support as a unified but highly varied *ecology of vocation*. In the variety of arenas suggested in the last chapter's
discussion of human partnership with divine action, members of the community form and reform the structure of vocational existence in their lives. Guided by the gifts they and
others perceive them to have and by the shape of human need
and the opportunities to serve, which they and the community discern, they give concrete form to purposes for their
lives that are part of the purposes of God in the world. In

these ways, the community of faith undertakes the risk of intentional cooperation in the emerging *divine praxis*.

Adequate development of each of these five levels of orientation and meaning by which communities of faith—and here, communities of Christian faith—awaken, form, and sustain vocational existence, would take another book. In this context, a few beginning observations on each will have to suffice.

3. THE CHRISTIAN STORY, PASSION, AND AFFECTIONS

The Community's Core Story. Much of the substance of what I would like to say about the Christian core story has already been suggested in Chapter IV's discussion of the narrative structure of the Christian classic. That must be coupled with the subsequent discussion in that chapter of the three Niebuhrian metaphors for discerning and responding to God's action in the world—God as Creator, God as Ruler, and God as Liberator-Redeemer. A tradition's core story represents its most comprehensive interpretation of the character of value and power in our ultimate environment and of its disposition to us. A religious core story enables us to see and comprehend our lives in relation to the life, history, and intentions of God. It provides a context of ultimate meaning for the events and relations of our lives; it gives us decisive images by which to interpret what we suffer and to sustain and guide us in what we hope. The Christian core story focuses in the love of Creator for created, in the decisive actions of Creator to restore relations with created, and to bring to glorious fulfillment the vision of an ultimate community of righteousness, love, and peace. To *see* God's sovereign action is to be called to partnership. This is partnership in love, in hope, in redemptive-liberative suffering, and in the incomparable joy and richness of communion with God and all creation.

The Community's Central Passion. Passions, in both Greek antiquity and the early Christianity deeply influenced by it, were typically thought of as strong eruptions of emotion in the service of the gratification of unworthy drives or needs. Passions threatened the resoluteness of the rational life; passions threatened the disciplines of the vowed monastic life. Passions (coming from the Greek *pathos*—suffering, usually bodily pangs; and the Latin *passio*, from *patior, passus*—to bear, to suffer) can, of course, refer to strong emotions of either a positive or negative sort: "A strong feeling or emotion by which the mind is swayed, as ambition, avarice, revenge, fear, hope, joy, grief, love, hatred." More consonant with the older cluster of meanings mentioned is "a strong, deep feeling; violent agitation or excitement of mind; violent anger; zeal, ardor, vehement desire. . .," and so on.

In referring to the central *passion* of the Christian master story, it is my intention to claim a symbol that holds together in a remarkable convergence some of the key elements of the heart of the Christian gospel.[6] First, it refers to the *passio*, the suffering of God in becoming flesh—the *incarnation*. "Bearing the human likeness, revealed in human shape, he humbled himself, and in obedience accepted even death—death on a cross" (Philippians 2:8, NEB). Second, it refers to the passion of God, which came to expression first in creation, then in the various covenants, and most decisively in the Christ event, for reconciled unity with and fulfillment of those created in the divine image. This is passion in the sense of deep longing, abiding love, and costly risking of the self. Third, it refers to the passion for the commonwealth of love (traditionally, Kingdom of God) that animated Jesus' preaching and teaching and that he saw as the inauguration of a new age to culminate in a faithful and universal Israel. This is passion in the sense of committed zeal, the enthusiastic giving of all that one is and has. And fourth, it refers to the identification with the passion of God in Christ, in *all* the previous senses, which becomes, by identification, the *raison d'être* of the church. Dietrich Bonhoeffer once wrote that "The church is nothing but a section of humanity in which Christ has really taken form."[7] That means, in this context, being formed by the passion of Christ. It means an entering into and a taking on of an identification with the passion of Christ so profound that it becomes the animating and prioritizing center of our corporate life.

A Christian Formation of Affections. The term *affections* employed as I am using it here was more characteristic of the eighteenth century than it is of the twentieth. It means "emotions" but not emotions in the contemporary, shallow sense of transient clusters of feelings or labile moods. Rather, it means emotions in the sense of a *deep-going, pervasive, and long-lasting set of fundamental dispositions of the heart.* In relation to our previous discussion of the central passion of the Christian faith, Christian affections are the deep dispositions and the emotional restings of the heart that result from one's devotion to that center. The Christian affections are close to what Saint Paul referred to in Galatians 5:22–25 (NEB) and elsewhere as "the harvest of the Spirit."

But the harvest of the Spirit is love, joy, peace, patience, kindness, goodness, fidelity, gentleness, and self-control. There is no law dealing with such things as these. And those who belong to Christ Jesus have crucified the lower nature with its passions and desires. If the Spirit is the source of our life, let the Spirit also direct our course.

Saint Paul speaks here on the basis of a psychology that will represent a dominant strain in Western theology and philosophy until the eighteenth century. The works of Saint Augustine, Luther, Calvin, Jonathan Edwards, and many others follow him in seeing that a person's intellect, reason, and the other abilities and talents at his/her disposal will be ordered in the service of his/her central love or devotion. As Jonathan Edwards put it, "The will is as its strongest motive is." Martin Luther put it more crudely: "Reason is a whore who will serve any master." In this psychology, the affections play a central role. The deep emotions determine the values, the purposes, and the ends for which human intelligence and energy will be mobilized.

Building on the classical list of the fruits of the Spirit in Saint Paul, contemporary theologians have sought to recover and reemphasize the centrality of the emotions in the life of faith. Among others, my colleague Don Saliers has taught me a great deal about the formation of what he takes to be a pattern of explicitly Christian emotions. In a recent book, *The Soul in Paraphrase*,[8] Saliers identifies four major clusters of Christian affections: (1.) gratitude and giving thanks, (2.) holy fear and repentance, (3.) joy and suffering, and (4.) the love of God and neighbor.[9] It is important to underline one of the sentences we quoted from Paul's writing in Galatians: "There is no law dealing with such things as these." Affections such as these are by-products of the will's attraction and commitment to the gracious love of God. They represent "habits of the heart" shaped by the human response in love, awakened by the power of Spirit.

Gratitude and giving thanks describe the deep disposition arising from our realizing that the world, our lives, and the lives of others are gracious gifts. Shaped by the beauty and the incomparable intricacy and extensiveness of the universe and by the wonder that we, or indeed anything at all, should *be,* gratitude affirms that *all* is grace. This is not to be confused with a bubbling chatter about "how good the Lord is," emoted primarily when we are at the peak of our youth or in the springtime of our lives. Giving thanks, as a pervasive affection, steadfastly and radiantly affirms the goodness of God, in the face of disappointment, disaster, and even of death itself.

Holy fear and repentance capture the deep emotions that reflect our awareness of the grandeur of God and of our infinite distance from God. I always think here of Isaiah in the temple, as reported in the sixth chapter of Isaiah, where in the majestic presence of God he said:

"Woe is me! I am lost,
for I am a man of unclean lips
and I dwell among a people of unclean lips;
yet with these eyes I have seen the King, the Lord
of Hosts. (Isaiah 6:5, NEB)

Isaiah suffered here from what my first college professor of Bible, Barney Jones, called "axiological alienation." Axiology has to do with *value;* alienation has to do with *separation* and being *sundered.* Isaiah saw himself in relation to the Glory of God. In the presence of the infinite center and source of all value, he felt his relative worthlessness and the infinite qualitative distance that alienated him from such goodness. Under the impact of this awareness, there is no alternative but repentance: a turning toward the source of love and light and a radical plea for the gift of being joined to God.

The third cluster of Christian affections identified by Don Saliers is *joy and suffering.* He reminds us that "Christian faith is born in the tension of suffering and joy, of cross and resurrection. The language of joy and of rejoicing we receive in Scripture must always be read against the backdrop of the life of suffering."[10] It is utterly authentic, therefore, when, in the middle of his joyous and celebrative Christmas oratorio, Johann Sebastian Bach includes the sonorous (and otherwise ominous) strains of "Oh Sacred Head Now Wounded." Reminding us that Christian prayer, patterned after Jesus' prayer for the Kingdom, is eschatological, Saliers says, "It anticipates the fullness of joy in the Kingdom which liberates us from our inordinate loves and desires in the world . . . (and) frees us from unhappiness and despair in the disappointments, pains, and sufferings of our existence." Then Saliers offers a strong paragraph on the realism of the emotions of joy and suffering in Christian faith:

This kind of joy is a condition for making sense of human existence. It is set at odds with our normal run of enjoyments and joys. Jesus remarks that in the world his followers will have tribulation, but nevertheless are to be of good cheer, for "I have overcome the world." This is not done through mere courage. Courage may be called for in the exercise of faith, but the joy is not a function of the will. Rather we are to welcome the world with its pain and suffering because it is into that world that God's glory comes in the form of a servant. To ignore the suffering of the world in the name of gratitude and joy violates and trivializes the message of Christianity . . . The joy of the resurrection is a sham without the agony of Gethsemane and the reality of the cross. To be afflicted in the world where powers of life and death contend is precisely our identification with the redemptive and suffering love of God in Christ . . . This is a strange and terrible beauty which draws us to a joy the world cannot know or give.[11]

We conclude our consideration of "A Christian Formation of Affections" with a brief look at the fourth cluster of specifically Christian emotions Saliers identifies—*the love of God and neighbor.* Here our account is a transition to what will follow, a discussion of the *virtues* required by the Christian community's *praxis.* The love of God and neighbor are so central to Christianity and to the Judiasm that formed Jesus of Nazareth that commentary is almost extraneous. However, to consider them as emotions—as Christian affections—is to see that they are not reducible to the status of moral principles, as though they were equivalent to Kant's categorical imperative in one or another of its formulations. To say that the love of God and neighbor are gracious affections is to affirm that they become in the Christian community, when it is faithful, a deep *habitus,* a pervasive orientation to the divine initiative and universality in love, leading its bearers to an empowered love for all that God loves. Gustav Wingren, in his great book *Luther on Vocation,* writes, "This is Christian love, in which man serves all who are needy, forgives his enemies, prays for all, and willingly suffers wrong. Love is inner willingness to do and to bear all that is required by vocation, but it does it gladly and without resistance; indeed, it willingly exceeds what is called for."[12]

The following lines represent the most moving illustration I know of the power of the affections of religious life, whether Christian or Jewish, to transform the hearts of human beings. Taken from the inner walls of one of the concentration camps in Nazi Germany at the end of the Second World War, this prayer was scratched by an unknown hand:

O Lord, when I shall come with glory into your kingdom, do not remember only the men of good will; remember also the men of evil. May they be remembered not only for their acts of cruelty in this camp, the evil they have done to us prisoners, but balance against their cruelty the fruits we have reaped under the stress and in the pain; the comradeship, the courage, the greatness of heart, the humility and patience which have been born in us and become part of our lives, because we have suffered at their hands.

May the memory of us not be a nightmare to them when they stand in judgment. May all that we have suffered be acceptable to you as a ransom for them.

And then the writing concluded, "Unless a grain of wheat falls into the ground and die . . ."[13]

This is joy and suffering; this is the love of God and neighbor.

4. VIRTUES AND VOCATION

We have given attention to three of the five interrelated levels by which a Christian community awakens and forms vocation in persons. We have examined "The Community's Core Story," "The Community's Central Passion," and "A Christian Formation of Affections." It may have occurred to the reader that in addition to clarifying these levels of orientation and formation in Christian community, we have also been identifying and elaborating elements in the makeup of Christian adulthood and maturity. Let us bring this section to a conclusion now by looking at the last two levels and elements: "The Virtues Required by the Community's Praxis" and "The Shaping and Reshaping of Personal Vocation."

The Virtues Required by the Community's Praxis. Alasdair MacIntyre makes it clear in his important book, *After Virtue,* that virtues take form and come to be valued in relation to a particular people's or culture's *social praxis.*[14] As I explained earlier, the term *social praxis* refers to the characteristic patterns of action and reaction by which a social group conducts its affairs and pursues its mission. Virtues, in this sense then, are strengths of personhood— capacities for discernment, judgment, and action; capacities for learning, cooperation, and leadership—that have moral significance. By *moral* significance, I mean to suggest two things: (1.) that the strengths in question are or become consistent qualities of persons that are therefore constitutive of their characters and intrinsic to their identities and (2.) that the strengths in question are valued in the community of shared praxis because they are perceived to be the fruits of commitment to the community's collective vocation and instrumental to the effective service of its central passion.

As in the case of Christian affections, the ancient and modern lists of so-called Christian virtues have significant variations. There are older religious and nonreligious conceptions of virtue that have influenced the Christian community's efforts, in various times and cultural settings, to define the moral strengths of persons requisite for Christian praxis. Saint Augustine is representative in this respect, with his effort to "convert" the classical Greek and Stoic notions of virtue to be expressive of the quality of moral strength called for by Christian praxis:

As to virtue leading us to a happy life, I hold virtue to be nothing else than perfect love of God. For the fourfold division of virtue I regard as taken from four forms of love. For these four virtues (would that all felt their influence in their minds as they have their names in their mouths!), I should have no hesitation in defining them: that temperance is love giving itself entirely to that which is loved; fortitude is love readily bearing all things for the sake of the loved object; justice is love serving only the loved object, and therefore ruling rightly; prudence is love distinguishing with sagacity between what hinders it and what helps it. The object of this love is not anything, but only God, the chief good, the highest wisdom, the perfect harmony. So we may express the definition thus: that temperance is love keeping itself entire and incorrupt for God; fortitude is love bearing everything readily for the sake of God; justice is love serving God only, and therefore ruling well all else, as subject to man; prudence is love making a right distinction between what helps it towards God and which might hinder it."[15]

Traditionally, the four classic virtues built upon here have been designated as the "cardinal virtues" in Christian theology and moral philosophy. In the Catholic tradition, they were taken to be "natural," part of the realization of the potential given to humans in God's creation. These were contrasted to what were called the "theological virtues"—faith, hope, and love. While the former were taken to be fruits of natural growth and development, the latter were considered to be the work of supernatural grace transforming and completing, in sanctification, the human potential for experiencing the restoration of the divine *imago*. The so-called theological virtues, the fruit of the work of Grace and Spirit, transformed, re-established, and redirected, the cardinal virtues.[16]

More recently, as the eschatological thrust of Jesus' teaching and preaching have been recovered and as the centrality of the proclamation of the in-breaking Kingdom of God in his message has been appreciated, theological ethicists have spoken more in terms of the eschatological character of Christian virtues. These accounts, often under the influence of Protestant understandings of the radicality of sin, stress more the *discontinuities* between human "natural" virtues and those strengths of personhood resulting from believers' responses to the inauguration of the new age made visible in the in-breaking commonwealth of love. In this context, Christian virtues become the "eschatological virtues"—the qualities of moral strength, skill, and capacity that enable the community to respond with courage, resourcefulness, and world-transforming effectiveness to the invitations and imperatives of the new age.

Bernard Häring's account of the eschatological virtues reveals a confusion regarding the distinction between *affections* and *virtues*.[17] His listing overlaps considerably what I, following Saliers and others, have designated as Christian affections; (1.) gratitude—humility, (2.) the creativity of hope, (3.) vigilance, and (4.) serenity and joy. It should be pointed out, however, that Häring discusses these virtues in the context of considering the Christian "fundamental option," a traditionally Catholic way of speaking of the life-defining commitment of faith. This fundamental option would include, and build upon, as we saw in Saint Augustine, the undergirding and permeative love of and for God.

More helpful, though less traditional, is the approach taken by Protestant theologian Daniel Jenkins.[18] In a chapter attempting to delineate the qualities of Christian maturity, he draws on both the Sermon on the Mount and the letters of Saint Paul. He lists: (1.) *Meekness,* by which he means the quality of gentle strength, controlled by the love of God and a hunger for righteousness. (2.)

Being a peacemaker, by which he means tending to those qualities in persons and community that contribute to *health;* guarding relationships in community and the public so as to produce peace; getting to the roots, not just the symptoms, of violence in the world. (3.) *Generosity,* meaning the qualities of spending and being spent for others because one is not anxious, on the one hand, and is filled with gratitude, on the other. (4.) *Magnanimity,* for which the Greek (Pauline) term is *Epieikeia,* meaning "largeness of spirit." Jenkins seems here to mean getting beyond pettiness and undue concern for things of little consequence. In the eschatological context in which all of these virtues are meant to be understood, *Epieikeia* means a forebearance, a tolerance, an active focusing on the truly important issues, in light of the invitations and imperatives of the in-breaking new age. (5.) *Joyfulness,* here not primarily referring to the emotions or affections of joy but to the capacity to live with joy, to *make* celebration; the capacity (freedom and skill) to *play* as an anticipation of the freedom, spontaneity, and joy of the new age; the capacity to bring this quality of festivity and play to the work and care for a world of struggle, suffering, and bleared *not-yet.*

Notice that Jenkins's discussion deals with virtues both as qualities of persons and of communities. His perspective is extremely valuable because he takes seriously the issues, discussed in the first part of this chapter, that arise in communities where motivations of destiny and self-groundedness are mixed with motives of vocation and covenant, both in the community and in individual persons. Jenkins's discussion helps us to see that skills of community building and maintenance, of organizational decision making and conflict resolution, and of hospitality and public policy formation are closely related to and required for virtues in today's communities of Christian fatih. We will have more to say about matters of this kind as we turn, in a later section, to consider the mutual enrichment that adult development theories and concern with the virtues of Christian community can bring to each other.

The Shaping and Reshaping of Personal Vocation. To conclude, I want to return briefly to the concept of vocation. This represents the fifth and last level of informing orientations and meanings by which communities of faith awaken and shape vocational existence. What must be said of vocation in the lives of each member of the community of faith? And what must be said of their inter-relatedness in *an ecology of vocations?*

Mary Cosby of the Church of the Savior in Washington, D.C. says that one of the principal tasks of ministry in that community of faith is the discernment and calling forth of gifts.[19] In that community, the shaping of personal vocation is a matter of corporate discernment and imagination as much as it is a concern of the particular person involved. Earlier we talked of a "vocational adventure" to which each of us is called. Rather than thinking of one's vocation as a kind of Platonic ideal form, waiting for us somewhere in the future, this kind of approach to the question of vocation urges us to take a frankly "negotiational" stance. By that I mean an approach that combines giving attention to one's gifts and inclinations, with a careful listening to the Christian story and vision, both in dynamic relation to the structure of needs and opportunities presented by the surrounding world. Vocation, in this sense, is not "found" so much as it is *negotiated.* We shape "a purpose for our lives that is part of the purposes of God" by means of proposal and counterproposal, by means of inclination and the nudges or the real lures or shoves of the divine calling. Communities play a critical role in this process by providing relational contexts where we are known personally (over time), where we are taken seriously, and where we are invited to submit our images of ourselves and our vocations to trusted others, who are informed by the community's "script" and core story, for correction and/or confirmation. The community of faith, at its best, is an "ecology of vocations." In a microcosmic way, the Christian community is a sign and anticipation of a universal community in which our callings will be complementary and where our talents, energies, passions, affections, and virtues will coalesce in the praise and service of God.

NOTES

1. David Bakan, *The Duality of Human Existence* (Boston: Beacon Press, 1966), esp. pp. 102ff.
2. Walter Brueggemann, "Covenanting as Human Vocation," *Interpretation* 33: (2.), pp. 115–129.
3. Paul Tillich, *The Courage to Be* (New Haven: Yale University Press, 1952), chaps. 4–5.
4. I owe these insights to H. Richard Niebuhr, and through him to Josiah Royce.
5. C. B. Macpherson, *The Political Theory of Possessive Individualism: From Hobbes to Locke* (New York: Oxford University Press, 1962).
6. Though my treatment of these issues differs considerably from his, the work of Jürgen Moltmann on the *pathos* of God, in various of his writings (most notably, *The Trinity and the Kingdom of God*, [San Francisco: Harper & Row, 1981]) has been important for me.
7. Dietrich Bonhoeffer, *Ethics*, trans. Neville Horton Smith, 6th ed. (New York: Macmillan, 1955), p. 83.
8. Don Saliers, *The Soul in Paraphrase* (New York: Crossroad-Seabury Books, 1980).
9. Ibid., especially chap. 4.
10. Ibid., p. 68.
11. Ibid., pp. 69–70.
12. Gustav Wingren, *The Christian's Calling: Luther on Vocation* (Tr. by Carl C. Rasmussen) (Edinburgh: Tweaddale Court: Oliver and Boyd, 1958), p. 64.
13. From a personal communication from Ruth Rosenbaum. Source unknown.
14. Alasdair MacIntyre, *After Virtue* (Notre Dame: University of Notre Dame Press, 1981), chaps. 10–18.
15. From "On the Morals of the Catholic Church," chap. 15. Quoted in Waldo Beach and H. Richard Niebuhr, *Christian Ethics*, 2nd ed. (New York: Wiley, 1973), p. 115.
16. See Karl Rahner, "Virtue," in Karl Rahner, ed., *Encyclopedia of Theology: The Concise Sacramentum Mundi* (New York: Seabury, 1978), pp. 201–08.
17. Bernard Häring, *Free and Faithful in Christ* (New York: Seabury, 1978). vol. I, pp. 201–208.
18. Daniel Jenkins, *Christian Maturity and Christian Success* (Philadelphia: Fortress Press, 1982). See especially chap. 2. Despite its unfortunate title, this entire book is a rich background and supplement to the present volume.
19. Mary Cosby, public lecture, Wesleyan College, Macon, Georgia, Summer 1979.

VI. Becoming Adult, Becoming Christian

1. STUDIES IN VOCATION

Not long ago I spent three days as a visiting lecturer and consultant on the campus of a prestigious private southwestern university. During that time, I met and talked in some depth with a few faculty members from various departments. Our concerns were with curricular and extracurricular issues, faith development, and the university as a context for student growth. I particularly remember my talk with an able associate professor of history, a well-prepared man in his late thirties. He had explained to me, earlier in our talk, that many of the students he taught came from exceedingly affluent family backgrounds. A number of them, he pointed out, drove cars that cost more than the total of his annual salary. By way of a gentle jab, I asked him what good he hoped to do teaching history in a place like this and to students who would, in all likelihood, simply go back home after graduation and take over some big chunk of their family businesses. I shall never forget his answer. He drew himself up to his full vocational dignity and said, "I am a teacher of history. My field of expertise is nineteenth-century British labor movements. My purpose in teaching here is to use the subject matter of my field and the methods of my discipline to contribute all that I can to a process of detoxification for young men and women who are likely to be people of power and influence in this society and who all their lives have been mainlining on this culture's images of success and power."

Like Mr. Adams earlier in the book, this man's life has more dimensions than just his work at the university. And, of course, his work as a teacher includes many concerns besides teaching and research. But I felt, somehow, that in his brief, pointed answer, made in the face of a challenge to the integrity of his work, I got a clear window of vision into his vocation. He did not give, nor did I ask for, any account of how his vocation relates to the faith or religious stance he might claim. Yet one knew, by the manner he exhibited in the meeting and through our discussion of the purposes of teaching, that he was spending his life energies and using his special gifts and training in the service of a sense of truth that had captured him. One felt his hope that others could be awakened to a regard for that truth and equipped with methods and perspectives that would make them its inquiring instruments.

Time would fail me to write about other "ordinary people" whose vocations I have had the privilege of spying into. One could mention a retirement-aged woman—wife, grandmother, community educator and leader—pouring out her energies in sixteen-hour days in the service of humane and decent law in the state legislature. Or we could meet a slender man in his thirties, who spends his days as the warm and efficient operator of a university photo-offset copy service. Weekends and evenings, however, he can be found traveling and performing with the soul gospel group he organized and leads. The records he cuts and the concerts he sings, in churches and schools, probably cover the expenses. The income they produce has little to do, if I am any judge, with the reasons why he shares his talents and his faith. Then there is a postman, a letter carrier in a mountain town, who across thirty years has used his love for horses and a little farm he has as a means to help retrieve troubled youth from the brink of disaster and to help them envision alternatives.

We could go on. A brilliant medical teacher and administrator whose busy life of supervising and counseling students is balanced by the steady production of poems that sensitively probe and remind us of the shape of acute human vulnerability in gleaming hospital corridors. A wealthy junior leaguer, wife and mother of teenagers, pouring our her life in service to her church, in volunteer work, and in sitting on the boards of more community service, mental health, and social change agencies than we could count, decides in early mid-life to try to name and focus the vocational hunger underlying her activities. Now completing a rigorous program of study and apprenticeship in spiritual direction, she is beginning to share her gifts as counselor and director with other women who are seeking to identify and name their vocational hungers.

When we deal with the question of vocation, we are engaging ourselves in an area of great mystery and of great sacredness. There is truthfully nothing more sacred to a man or a woman than the meaning, the value, or the purpose in being of their lives. To be sure, persons can fall into numbness regarding these issues. They can suffer such obstacles and defeats regarding their bids to actualize their vocations that they give up in despair. Then they try to ease the pain through one form of narcotization or another. Numbness of another sort endangers those who find an avenue to wealth or power—or get obsessively caught up in the pursuit of such an avenue—to the extent that their sensitivities to the inner and outer voices of vocation become muted. Our times and our particular concatenation of cultural values make this kind of "seduction of the spirit" exceedingly strong and insidious.

It is a middle- and upper-class myth, however, that says that all a person needs successfully to pursue her/his vocation is determination, commitment, and a measure of luck and pluck. Using the methods of his teacher Daniel Levinson, Winston Gooden studied "the seasons of Black men's lives."[1] In his sample of fifteen men, Gooden included ten men who had achieved middle-class status or above. But he also included five "street men." What is most moving and disturbing about Gooden's fine study is its disclosure of the obstacles that poverty, a racist society, the legacy of slavery's brutalization of the family, and a lack of available mentors and sponsors placed in the way of those who became "street men." Gooden's study of the texture of these men's lives gives the lie to that pack of sentiments that says, in rationalizing the toleration of human deprivation and suffering, "They could get work if they wanted to. They deserve their plight." With bone-chilling regularity, Gooden documents how these five men formed one dream after another, often putting together many of the pieces required to get them launched. But then, through a combination of flawed planning or preparation, lack of mentoring and support, and the indifference or hostility of their environments, the scaffolding of their dreams collapsed. Like beaten boxers, these men, for an astonishingly long time, kept resurrecting, modifying, and struggling again with their dreams.

We have reflected so far on the patterns of vocation in the lives of what I, somewhat misleadingly, called "ordinary people." When we observe people who are in vocation—people who have found purposes for their lives that are part of the purposes of God —we are struck by just how *un*ordinary they seem. And yet, I believe that the quality of their engagement, their gladness in spending and being spent, and the creativity that characterizes these persons who are in vocation is somehow close to what, at best, it means to be a human being. That's why I have insisted that we consider not just the idea of *Christian* vocation but rather the Christian idea of the *human* vocation.

In the brief sketches of persons I have offered here, there have been only a few hints about their processes of discerning, responding to, and forming their vocations. One's awakening to vocation is related to, but not identical with, the early development of a sense of specialness or of worth. It also includes the awakening of desires and inclinations regarding the future uses and qualities of the self. Vocational self-discovery involves the awakening and forming of talents, sensibilities, and aptitudes. The presence or absence of significant others who can help us recognize and confirm our promise and our gifts are crucial in the beginning discernment of vocation. And among the most important factors contributing to the evolution of a sense of vocation is the feeling, conveyed either by those who are closest to us or gathered beyond and in spite of them, that *much is expected of us.*

The wonderful novel by Chaim Potok, *My Name Is Asher Lev,*[2] details the awakening and shaping of vocation in the life of an exceptionally gifted Jewish lad, born into a Ladover Hasidic family in Brooklyn in the late 1940s. The story, told with beautiful sensitivity to the way a thoughtful child experiences and interprets his world, draws into fine focus many of the central issues of this book. The Ladover Hasidic community, of which Asher Lev's parents are members, illustrates powerfully the five levels of orientation and meaning I characterized earlier as essential in communities of faith that would awaken and form a sense of vocation. The community is a true ecology of vocations.

Asher Lev's father, like his own father and grandfather before him, is a kind of ambassador for the Rebbe, the spiritual and governing head of the community. A political scientist by training, master of seven or eight languages, a devout ritual observant steeped in Talmud, and a loving husband and father, the senior Lev's passion centers in the re-establishment of Ladover Yeshivas (schools for Talmudic education) in the major cities of postwar Europe and in welcoming to them the refugee Ladovers from a persecuted Soviet Jewry. For this he pours out his life energy; for this he is willing to endure long separations from his wife and only son.

Asher Lev's mother, orphaned along with her sister and only brother at an early age, grieves terribly at the accidental death (when Asher Lev is four) of the brother. After a year of mourning and being near death, she takes the unusual vocational step, for an Orthodox woman, of asking the Rebbe for permission to attend university and to complete undergraduate and graduate degrees in Russian studies, so that she can take up the vocation of her deceased brother. In his agreeing to this proposal, the Rebbe shows his largeness of vision, his wisdom, and his flexibility.

Into this intense vocational cauldron Asher Lev is born, carrying within him the genes of a world-class artist. Remembering the strictures of ancient Judaism against making "graven images" and its acute awareness of the dangers of idolatry, the reader is led to recognize how problematic it is for the father and mother of Asher Lev and for the whole Ladover community to watch and welcome the unfolding of his extraordinary set of artistic gifts. Asher Lev early shows a remarkable genius with eye and hand for artistic representation. He is absorbed with drawing and painting, to the point that the parents and his teachers discourage him at ages seven or eight, and the sensitive boy abandons his talent for several years. Not until early adolescence does he experience the reawakening of the gift. At this age, now well able to grasp the theological issues at stake in the interpretation of his genius. Asher Lev feels it very deeply when his father expresses grave doubts whether his artistic giftedness is from *Ribbono Shel Olom*—the Master of the Universe—or from *sitra achra*—"the other side," the demonic.

In another gracious and wise act of sponsorship, the Rebbe arranges for Asher Lev to have tutoring in art from a great Jewish painter and sculptor, who himself had grown up in the Ladover community. Jacob Kahn had allowed formal ties of ritual practice and observing kosher to lapse. On conviction, he had made his experience of and commitment to artistic truth the center of his life. The drama of the novel builds to tremendous intensity as Asher Lev experiences the deepening conflict, within and about him, between his fidelity to the truth of Judaism—as embodied in Torah, his community, and his family—and his fidelity to his genius, and the gift and burden of painting truth. Asher Lev, like many persons of true genius who are also genuinely religious, wrestles profoundly with the question of whether his giftedness will ultimately serve the success and influence of a personal destiny or whether it will be developed no less fully but offered in vocational faithfulness.

The climactic paragraph of the book brings Asher Lev's terrible struggle to expression and discloses the resolution he comes to through the gift of divine grace. His second major exhibit, at age twenty, had been a striking critical and financial success. But it had included two paintings that portrayed, as though she were on a cross, the terrible emotional pulls his mother endured trying to hold together and mediate between Asher Lev and his obdurate father. The power of the crucifixion image in the two paintings scandalized the Hasids and crushed his parents. As we pick up Potok's text, Asher Lev has just been told by a sorrowful Rebbe that he has irrevocably crossed a boundary and that he must leave the congregation and his family. He is to go to the Ladover community in Paris, where he had built relationships during a recent year of painting in France. Coming to terms with this decree and with all that it portends, Asher Lev has walked for hours in the snow:

Sometime during the walking, I stopped in front of a mound of snow and with my finger drew in one continuous line the contour of my face. Asher Lev in snow on a cold Brooklyn parkway. Asher Lev, Hasid. Asher Lev, painter. I looked at my right hand, the hand with which I painted. There was power in that hand. Power to create and destroy. Power to bring pleasure and pain. Power to amuse and horrify. There was in that hand the demonic and the divine at one and the same time. The demonic and the divine were two aspects of the same force. Creation was demonic and divine. Creativity was demonic and divine. Art was demonic and divine . . . I was demonic and divine. Asher Lev, son of Aryeh and Rivkeh Lev, was the child of the Master of the Universe *and* the Other Side. Asher Lev paints good pictures and hurts people he loves. Then be a great painter, Asher Lev; that will be the only justification for all the pain you will cause. But as a great painter I will cause pain again if I must. Then become a greater painter. But I will cause pain again. Then become a still greater painter. Master of the Universe, will I live this way all the rest of my life? Yes, came the whisper from the branches of the trees, Now journey with me, my Asher. Paint the anguish of all the world. Let people see the pain. But create your own molds and your own play of forms for the pain. We must give a balance to the universe.[3]

2. VOCATION AND THE STORIES OF OUR LIVES

Some readers, remembering that this is a book about Christian adulthood, may find it surprisng that I concluded the previous section with a retelling of Potok's story of young Asher Lev. Please remember that our concern, throughout, has been to explicate a Christian perspective on the *human* vocation, as well as to clarify the passions, affections, and virtues with which Christian communities seek to fit persons for vocation. Besides reminding us of this double concern, the Lev story helps us in another crucial way: It helps us to see that the life of each of us is a story in progress—a story taking form and living out a narrative structure. Potok's novel shows promise of being a classic, I believe, precisely because it brings to expression, in ways that have universal appeal, our common experience of struggling to shape our stories in interaction with the vocational stories of others. Its significance as a classic is deepened and confirmed, moreover, because in addition to depicting the interliving of vocational existence within a family and community, it illumines the texture of vocational life lived in struggle with *Ribbono Shel Olom*—with the Master of the Universe. In its account of this struggle with God, the book keeps faith with the ambiguity of the demonic (daimonic) dynamics and potentials of our concerns with destiny and vocation. Though its contours are sharpened by the quality of Asher Lev's genius and by the strictness and clarity of his community's passion, his story illumines the character of our stories. His struggle focuses the essential dimensions of our narratives-in-progress, at least insofar as they engage issues of vocation and destiny.

Author Phyllis Rose captures something of the existential feel of our lives as lived narratives in the introduction to her book *Parallel Lives:*

I believe, first of all, that living is an act of creativity and that, at certain moments of our lives, our creative imaginations are more conspicuously demanded than at others. At certain moments, the need to decide upon the story of our own lives becomes particularly pressing—when we choose a mate, for example, or embark upon a career. Decisions like that make sense, retroactively, of the past and project a meaning onto the future, knit past and future together, and create, suspended between the two, the present. Questions we have all asked of ourselves such as Why am I doing this? or the even more basic What am I doing? suggest the way in which living forces us to look for and forces us to find a design within the primal stew of data which is our daily experience. There is a kind of arranging and telling and choosing of detail—of narration, in short— which we must do so that one day will prepare for the next day, one week prepare for the next week . . . To the extent that we impose some narrative form onto our lives, each of us in the ordinary process of living is a fitful novelist.[4]

Rose implicitly recognizes that our stories are interwoven with those of others. But reading her account, one could draw the inference that we have the initiative and the capacity largely to shape our stories-in-progress according to our desires or our personal constructions of meaning. It is not made so clear in what she has written that the stories we take ourselves to be living often collide and clash with the intended stories of others. Nor does her statement take account of the presence of the core stories of our traditions that precede our coming to consciousness and provide symbol, image, and story by which we awaken to the task of making meaning.

A passage from Alasdair MacIntyre, in the context of his writing about the narrative structure of our lives as moral agents, helps us to move further toward an adequate grasp of the dynamics of forming the vocational stories of our lives:

I spoke earlier of the agent as not only an actor, but an author. Now I must emphasize that what the agent is able to do and say intelligibly as an actor is deeply affected by the fact that we are never more (and sometimes less) than the co-authors of our own narratives. Only in fantasy do we live what story we please. In life, as both Aristotle and Engels noted, we are always under certain constraints. We enter upon a stage which we did not design and we find ourselves part of an action that was not of our making. Each of us being a main character in his own drama plays subordinate parts in the dramas of others, and each drama constrains the others. In my drama, perhaps, I am Hamlet or Iago or at least the swineherd who may yet become a prince, but to you I am only A Gentleman or at best Second Murderer, while you are my Polonius or my Gravedigger, but your own hero. Each of our dramas exerts constraints on each other's, making the whole different from the parts, but still dramatic.[5]

Adding MacIntyre's insights to those of Rose helps us to see that in the co-authorship of our life stories, the questions, at crucial points of self-defining commitment and action, press us back further than the analysis of our own motivations and actions. Finding ourselves on stages not of our own making and in the midst of actions not of our own design, the big question becomes, What is going on? In all of the actions clashing about me, is there some unifying action that contains, orders, and gives purpose and meaning to the whole? If so, how do I discern the pattern or intention of that action, and more, how do I shape my initiatives and my responses so as to make them *congruent* with it?

At this point, the animating purpose of this book can be brought into focus. In the present, any serious, intentional approach to helping persons and groups form their lives in accordance with the Christian story and vision has to coordinate the convergence of three vectors of meaning: (1.) the dynamism and direction of their personal life narratives, (2.) the web of social interchanges in time that constitute their evolving life structures, and (3.) the perspectives on the Divine praxis and purpose offered in the core story of the Christian faith. The word *convergence* here means to suggest a process of *interplay,* of *interaction,* of creative mutual *interpenetration* between these three vectors, which will prove transformative for persons in the direction of faithful and imaginative partnership with God.

The deep metaphor giving unity to this book is either that of a dance or of a drama, each of which has a narrative structure. The dynamism of the dance or drama, however, is open-ended. The stage on which it plays is the product, ever changing, of cocreation between unequals. The prime creator is, in some sense, simultaneously theater owner, producer, first author, director, and fellow participant in the action. We, in intergenerational tides, come onto the stage to learn our moves and to awaken to the dance or drama in process. In the whirl, in the stirring of subplots and counterplots, we find places in relation to others whose story about the larger story forms our movements and gives us clues to the larger action into which we try to fit the motions of our days and years. To be in vocation means to grow in a "grace-full" fitting of our dance to the larger movement of the core plot. To be in vocation means to make creative contributions to the ongoing unfolding of the drama, in accordance with the vision and denouement intended by the playwright. To be in vocation means to develop the talents and gifts one has been given *for the sake, and within the constraints, of enriching and moving the whole drama-dance toward the climactic fulfillment envisioned by the script.* To be in vocation also means to come to terms with the limits of personal endowments, the disadvantages of one's initial point of entry onto the stage, and the chaos or destructive brutality of some of the action and actors who may constitute the subplots into which we emerge. To be in vocation under these conditions means to know and trust that the actor-director is also present—in masked or hidden form—sharing, bearing, and working to redeem and restore this anarchic corner to the goals of the larger play.

Within the frame established by this elaborated metaphor, we can consider how the perspectives on human development and on the Christian story and Christian community, which this book offers, contribute to the convergence of vectors we called for earlier. In other words, we can try to bring into focus that dynamic interplay of personal story, corporate-social existence, and the narrative structure of the Christian story and vision, which lies at the heart of transformation from self-groundedness toward vocation.

3. DEVELOPMENT AND CONVERSION

The contributions of the adult development theories that we studied in Chapters II and III of this book come now at the point of helping us name and address some of the shared elements of our personal stories and the common features of our social and corporate existence. Taken as descriptive of certain predictable movements and changes in our experiences of adulthood, they provide something like a set of "every person's stories" that we can use to guide us in our consideration of the transforming dialectic between our stories and the Christian story. The underlying motion we will try to capture is that of transformation—transformation from self-groundedness toward vocation. Our task is made more complex, however, by the need to take account of the double dynamics involved in combining both conversion and development in the motion of transformation. Let me explain.

In the developmental perspectives of Erikson, Levinson, and Gilligan, development involves a movement of the self in time in which each stage or season brings new challenges requiring adaptive growth and change. In this process, these theorists suggest, a cumulative enrichening of the self can occur. Like a musical group that continues to expand the range and diversity of its instruments while steadily working to master the new music that their new range allows, the reportoire of a person's abilities and flexibility increases. This is one set of developmental dynamics we need to keep in mind as we look at adult transformation toward vocation.

The faith development perspective on adulthood calls our attention to a somehwat different, but equally important, set of developmental dynamics. Unlike the psychosocial theorists of the previous paragraph, the faith stage perspective does not see developmental movement in the sense of stage change as coming automatically or inevitably with the passage of time and the changing of our bodies or of our social roles. In this constructive-developmental perspective, development means undergoing a qualitative change in the operations of knowing, committing, and valuing, by which one constructs the kind of narrative of meaning that our earlier quote from Phyllis Rose suggested. In this perspective, we reconstruct our *ways* of being in faith when we encounter disruptions or sources of dissonance in our personal or collective lives that our previous ways of making meaning cannot handle. The emergence of a new stage means the altering of previous ways of believing and understanding; it means constructing more inclusive, more internally complex, and more flexible ways of appropriating the contents—the substance and narrative power—of one's religious tradition.

It is important to see that in neither of the senses of development I have just described does one *necessarily* take a step away from self-groundedness and toward vocation. In neither of the types of development represented by the psychosocial theorists or by faith development theory is development *necessarily* tied to the recentering of one's passion, the realigning of one's affections, or the restructuring of one's virtues. Development, as described in both these perspectives, *can* be a movement that simply makes an attitude of self-groundedness more sophisticated, more skillful, and more entrenched. Development can mean simply a more effective and more single-minded pursuit of one's sense of individual or group destiny.

The transformation toward vocation of which we speak requires not only development but also *conversion*. By conversion, here, I do not mean simply some dramatic experience of conviction and release that occurs once, after which things have forever been made right. Rather, by conversion I mean *an ongoing process*— with, of course, a series of important moments of perspective-altering convictions and illuminations—*through which people (or a group) gradually bring the lived story of their lives into congruence with the core story of the Christian faith*. Conversion means a release from the burden of self-groundedness. It means accepting, at a depth of the heart that is truly liberating, that our worth, our value, our grounding as children of God is *given* as our birthright. It means embracing the conviction that we are known, loved, supported, and invited to partnership in being with One, who from all eternity intended us and who desires our love and friendship. Conversion means a recentering of our passion. It is a falling in love with the God who became like us and who invites and empowers us to a relation like that of parent to adult son or daughter. It means making an attachment to the passion of Jesus the Christ—a loving, committed, and ready-to-suffer passion for the in-breaking commonwealth of love. Conversion means a realignment of our affections, the restructuring of our virtues, and the growth in lucidity and power of our partnership with God's work in the world.

Conversion, then, is not so much a negation of our human development as it is a transformation and fulfillment of it. It is not so much a denial of our adulthood as it is the liberation and empowerment of our adulthood toward partnership with God. Conversion does not mean the negation of our sense of specialness and destiny so much as it means a radical regrounding of both, drawing them into the movement of a much larger drama that can call forth all the potential for greatness and heroism in service that any of us has been given.

The Christian approach to the transformation from self-ground-edness to vocational existence involves, then, the affirmation of *both* development and conversion. The spiritual traditions of the Eastern Orthodox branch of the Christian community have a special way of describing the process of ongoing conversion by which God rectifies and realigns human development. They speak of the gracious gift of a divine "synergy" working with and bringing to wholeness and completion our potentials and their development. Synergy means cauterization and healing of our tendencies to self-groundedness. Synergy means the mingling of divine love with our capacities to love, guiding them and grounding them in the grace of God. Synergy means the release of a quality of creativity and energy that manifests our likeness to the restored image of God in us. Synergy means human beings fully alive and using the gift of our strengths and virtues in the service of the realization of the commonwealth of love. In the Western Christian church, there has been greater caution in speaking of anything like the gift of divine synergy. This is due to a fear that we might fail radically enough to face the depths and inescapability of our fallen-ness and of our immersion in the alienation of sin. In the Western traditions, among those thinkers who have taken this idea seriously, it has been taught in terms of the *sanctifying* work of God's grace. We cannot afford to be without the "hermeneutics of suspicion" that have their root in this strong Western doctrine of original sin. But in our present situation of confusion and ferment regarding images of human wholeness and completion, we are in *critical* need of a theory of transformation and development that takes account of the power and availability to us of the synergy of God's grace.

4. BECOMING ADULT, BECOMING CHRISTIAN

Adult development theories point to certain expectable times of transition in our lives. These can be times when we will be engaged in moving from one season of our lives to another. Or they can be times when a particular crisis, associated with a given age or stage, demands our conscious and unconscious attention. Perspectives on adult development alert us to the fact that, with these seasonal movements, we will be testing, shaping, and re-forming the ways we relate to others and the world, as well as revising the ways in which we image ourselves. When we consider the dynamics of faith in our lives, we sense that at each of the crisis points of our lives and at each of the expected or unexpected turning points of our lives, we face a time when our ways of making meaning and the patterns of our trusts and loyalties are subject to testing and change. We are getting used to the idea that adulthood is not static. We are coming to terms with the insight that change is normative, continuous, and consequential.

How shall we bring together—in our understandings, and more importantly, in our lives—the perspectives of vocation and Christian conversion with the perspectives of psychosocial and faith development? How shall we put together, in practical terms, the possibilities of both development and conversion? How can we bring together both our psychological and our theological-ethical insights into destiny and vocation, into human development and divine calling?

Young Adulthood and the Vocational Dream. Let me say at the outset that in young adulthood, it is very difficult indeed to sort out and clarify issues of destiny and vocation. I wept during my one year of teaching undergraduates at Boston College as I came to terms with how few of my 260 or so students had any sense of themselves as *truly* special, as gifted, or as people of destiny *or* vocation. Since then, I have been especially sensitive to how hard it is, how frightening it is for young adults to move with assurance and hope into the adult world of work, commitments, and relationships. The transience of our communities, the complexity of highly specialized technologies, and the vagueness of the vocational profiles that many of their elders project make it exceedingly difficult to form a *dream,* in Levinson's sense. The dream, you remember, is a projected vision of the self into the future that can guide, nerve, and sustain a young man or woman in moving into the structures of today's adult living. The formation of a dream is further complicated by the forbidding presence of the nuclear threat—a factor from birth for today's young adults. This threat constitutes a grave backdrop against which the question of whether they will ever reach forty makes a great deal of sense.

The challenge and invitation the Christian community has to offer late adolescents and young adults is that of shaping their young adult dream in terms of vocation. To offer this challenge and invitation will mean to surround youth and young adults with a counterculture—an alternative consciousness. The voices inviting them to destiny dreams are powerful and attractive. Most frequently, those offering destiny dreams give advice. They say things like: Be sure to major in something marketable. Get a background that combines business and a specialty in computer technology—that's where all the growth is going to be. When you join your first company, keep your resumé always ready. If you are going to get to the top, you have got to be within striking distance by the time you are thirty-five; you have no time to dillydally or investigate other possibilities. Don't stay with any one company too long; loyalty can be counterproductive if you really want to get ahead. If you are going to be a top scientist or mathematician, you don't have time for volunteer activities—you've got to make every moment count. If you are going to get into a good medical school, you have no time to take "soft" courses like literature or philosophy.

Invitations to vocation dreams, on the other hand, are more likely to ask questions: What seem to be your gifts? What kinds of things do you do well? What kinds of activities and contributions really give you a sense of worthiness? What kinds of things do you find most challenging and fulfilling to do? In what kind of activities do you feel that you are most yourself? What kind of people do you most admire and would you particularly like to count among your associates? Do you feel an inner nudge or call that seems to be pointing you in some particular direction? What kinds of things do you feel that you and God can do with your life that will make a difference for good in our world?

The psychoanalyst Otto Kernberg has written an interesting chapter called "Normal Narcissism in Middle Age."[6] His principal point in this rich essay is that for vital growth and renewal to occur in middle life, a person has to make a healthy investment in him or herself and require that others do so as well. Similarly, the young adult who is engaged in trying to discern and shape a vocational dream is likely to exhibit a self-involvement that can look and seem narcissistic. The books that Erik Erikson has written on troubled youth and young adults who later became epoch-making adults (Luther, Jefferson, Gorky, Bernard Shaw, and Gandhi) have really been concerned not so much with *identity* as with *vocation*. (Recall Brueggemann's statement that a covenantal perspective transposes all identity questions into *vocational* questions.) The Christian community, if it intends to call and support young men and women in negotiating their ways toward vocation, will need to provide images and communal encouragement to resist both the panic and the seductions of the spirit that come from a society that mainly knows about specialness only in terms of destiny. But it will also need to provide more: In its testimony to its faith, in its communal fidelity through the vocations of its members, *it must witness to the faithfulness and power of a providential God who invites, helps to shape, and invests in active partnership with those who genuinely seek to respond to their callings.*

The miracle of vocation lies here. The transcendent Lord of history, the Creator, Ruler, and Redeemer-Liberator of the Universe promises and can be counted on to include in partnership men and women who with all their hearts seek to respond to their callings. Here and in later stages as well, the Christian community needs to offer a spirituality of vocation that can nerve young women and men against panic and seduction, on the one hand, and stand with them in discerning the shape of their callings in light of their gifts, the needs of the world, and the structures of opportunity and creativity that confront them, on the other. It can be a highly significant part of the vocations of middle and older adults to come to know, invest in, and support the awakening and forming of vocation in persons in the period from their late teens to their early thirties. This is to be a mentoring and sponsoring community. There is no higher or more sacred privilege.

Middle Adulthood: The Purification and Deepening of Vocation. In the years from roughly age twenty-eight to forty, Levinson indicates that adults can expect to have one or more periods of turmoil and vocational questioning. Please remember that I am using *vocation* here in a more comprehensive sense than just work, job, or profession. With Levinson, I am referring to times when the personal life structure has to be examined, re-evaluated, and either modified, extended, or confirmed. These times of vocational questioning are critical moments for the shaping of our life narratives. To think of them in terms of vocation is to recognize that in the moments when the fabric of our lives becomes torn or the texture of our lives is broken open, we become available in fresh ways to the calls or nudges of Spirit. These become times when we can stand to listen to the hungers of our hearts; they are moments when we may be apprehended for a new quality or direction of partnership.

By the time we enter our fifth decade, either we have lived through a number of such opening and re-forming times or we are prime candidates for a major encounter with vocational clarification. The forties bring the awareness that we have likely lived half our lives or beyond. We have moved in the world of adults long enough to have seen behind the curtains of the Wizard of Oz. Having lived with ourselves as adults for twenty years or more, we have had ample opportunity to come to terms with what horizons will likely define our lives and what ranks of power and influence are reasonable in our aspirations. We have thrilled and suffered with our young adult dreams and/or with those of our spouses and friends. Some parts of them have been fulfilled; other parts have been tattered, neglected, or forgotten. If we have been observant and reflective at all, we simply know things now— about ourselves, about the world, about our closest companions, and maybe about what things are *really* important—that we could not and did not know in our twenties or in our thirties.

The hunger for vocational purification and deepening at mid-life can reveal itself in a variety of symptoms and forms. A great deal of what we have come to call "burn-out" can be traced to the protests of souls whose vocational longings have for too long been ignored, suppressed, or violated. Many of the symptoms of "mid-life crisis," including marital unrest, job dissatisfaction, and other kinds of unaccountable restlessness, can be traced to anxiety and dread arising from the failure of the promises of our adolescent and young adult sense of destiny. Whether we have failed to achieve the goals that we thought would vindicate our destinies or whether we have achieved them and found that they have failed us, the real void comes from the discovery that the strategy of self-groundedness is an inadequate basis for our lives.

For both women and men, mid-life brings the invitations of deepening the spiritual foundations of our lives and of readdressing the issue of partnership with the Transcendent. Forms of spirituality that embrace the polarities and paradoxes of Conjunctive faith invite us to attend in new ways to the movements of Spirit within and between us and to the movements of Truth in our traditions. Having found the limits of self-groundedness as the basis for our lives, strangely we are open in new ways to falling in love with the true Ground of our Being. Development and conversion to the love and compassion of God are particularly likely to occur together in the lives of those who, at mid-life, have had to face the shame and painful self-knowledge that come when actions and directions they embarked upon to fulfill and actualize themselves have proven injurious to those they love and destructive of values to which they are committed. Development at mid-life often requires that we have our noses rubbed in the structures of self-deception that were, in earlier periods of our lives, part of what we perceived to be our strengths.

Older Adulthood: Witnesses and Guarantors of Vocation. There is an impressive quality of dignity, courage, and energy in the lives of those older adults who have found and been faithful to purposes for their lives that are part of the purposes of God. They exhibit the fruits of the kind of generativity Erikson writes about. They manifest a life-giving balance between a genuine being-for-others and a healthy regard for what faithfulness to their own callings requires. They have discovered, it seems, that partnership with God's work in the world does not lead to boredom and that vocational existence does not necessarily mean doing the same round of activities all one's life. Freed from the burden of justifying their lives with their works and liberated from the intensifying cycle of self-absorption that obsessive self-actualization requires, they have the internal freedom to take new risks and to initiate new roles and projects. In them we see, to a culminating degree, a quality that should emerge with verve in any season of our lives when we are in conversion from self-groundedness to vocation: a quality of playfulness and humor that arises from a love for persons that sees in them the kinds of persons God is calling them to be. This quality is close to genius—the kind of genius that, in its passion to know and understand, takes the time required to let that which is to be known have the initiative and meet us on its terms.

These qualities of elders in vocation give credibility and truth to their stories of vocational adventure. These qualities give weight to their testimonies of God's faithfulness in meeting us in vocation. These qualities give them authority when they confirm and encourage those on the threshold of vocation or those struggling in the vocational midstream. They thus become witnesses and guarantors of vocation. They are to us living signs of a faithful divine readiness powerfully and graciously to include us in the covenant partnership of a transforming synergy and love.

NOTES

1. Winston Gooden, "The Adult Development of Black Men" (Ph.D. diss., Yale University, 1980).
2. Chaim Potok, *My Name Is Asher Lev* (New York: Ballantine Fawcett Crest Book, 1973. 1983).
3. Ibid., p. 348.
4. Phyllis Rose, *Parallel Lives: Five Victorian Marriages* (New York: Knopf, 1983), pp. 5–6.
5. Alasdair MacIntyre, *After Virtue* (Notre Dame: University of Notre Dame Press, 1981), pp. 198–99.
6. Otto Kernberg, M.D., *Internal World and External Reality* (New York: Jason Aronson, 1980), pp. 121–34.

Acknowledgments

The materials now included in Chapters I to IV of this book have been lectured and taught in various stages to a number of audiences since 1981. I am grateful for the opportunities for discussion and critique afforded by teaching this material at Princeton Theological Seminary, Boston College, Kirkridge, and Ring Lake Ranch, as well as in my own classes at Candler School of Theology. Parts of the first four chapters were given under the following lectureships: the Cecil Lauer Lectures at McCormick Seminary; the Willson Lectures at Oklahoma City University; the Norton Lectures at Southern Baptist Theological Seminary; the Morgan Lectures at Lutheran Southern Theological Seminary; the McFadden Lectures at Brite Divinity School; the Finch Lectures at High Point College; the Spring Lectures at Southeastern Baptist Theological Seminary; and the Summer Lecture Series in Religious Education at Newman College, Birmingham, England. Versions of material in Chapters V and VI were given at Northwest Christian College; the Arrington Lectures at University of the South; and the Wieand Lectures at Bethany Theological Seminary. For the unfailing hospitality and stimulating engagement with friends in each of these settings, I am grateful.

This book is dedicated to two great mentors and friends. James Luther Adams, professor of religious ethics (emeritus) at Harvard Divinity School, was my major professor in my doctoral studies in religion and society. His course on "The Christian Doctrine of Vocation" was an early stimulus for the issues of this book, and his life is an extraordinary instance of the fullness and fruits of partnership with divine praxis. Carlyle Marney, special beyond words to me from my age seventeen till his death in 1978 (I was thirty-eight), wrote, taught, preached, and lived these themes with uncommon creativity and grace.

During the three years this book was taking form, so was the Center for Faith Development. I am deeply indebted to my associate director and friend, Romney Moseley, whose leadership of the Center Seminar provided rich intellectual stimulation and whose serving as acting director freed time to write. Richard Osmer of our staff taught his teachers well as we studied hermeneutics and David Tracy's work in the seminar. Stuart McLean, of Phillips University, was a fellow of the center during much of this writing. His discussion of these issues, his probing engagement of faith development theory, and his reading of parts of the manuscript are much appreciated. Staff member Dave Jarvis and Center Fellow Anne Mayeaux both made significant contributions to my effort to redescribe the stage of Universalizing faith, as did my friend and teaching assistant Lory Skwerer. Mary Lou McCrary of our staff helped greatly through proofreading the whole and giving editorial suggestions—and by protecting the author from the phone.

My wife, Lurline, keeps on becoming as a beloved partner in our shared vocational adventure. My thanks to and for her, always.

Index